CW00865022

ENEMIES UNITED

by

Barbara Anne Machin

Published by New Generation Publishing in 2021

Copyright © Barbara Anne Machin 2021

First Edition

The author asserts the moral right under the Copyright, Designs and Patents Act 1988 to be identified as the author of this work.

All Rights reserved. No part of this publication may be reproduced, stored in a retrieval system or transmitted, in any form or by any means without the prior consent of the author, nor be otherwise circulated in any form of binding or cover other than that which it is published and without a similar condition being imposed on the subsequent purchaser.

All the characters and names in this book are fictitious, and any resemblance to actual persons, living or dead, is purely coincidental.

ISBN   978-1-80031-236-4

www.newgeneration-publishing.com

New Generation Publishing

Chapter 1

The villagers of Brixham in England going about their daily business stopped to look and wonder what was glittering on the skyline. It appeared to be something that stretched along the whole horizon and bobbed up and down with the rough sea. It was so far away they couldn't make it out. The next day, there was a whole fleet of ships anchored on the water. They had sailed from Normandy to England and had disembarked their cargo of supplies and horses.

Seven hundred ships had sailed from Normandy later than they had expected to. William of Normandy had the Papal banner around his neck and the blessing of the pope to take his place on the English throne. Even though Harold had been elected by the witans as the king of England, William was to force his right to replace King Harold, who ruled the Saxon land. William also claimed he was the rightful king of England as he too had been promised the English throne. They had broken their promise, so William decided to take it by force.

The fleet had planned to sail in September, but strong winds and rough seas had forced them to wait. So, William had arrived on the English shores of Brixham on the fourteenth of October 1066.

Three days later, King Harold met his fate at the battle of Hastings. Wealthy thegns left their lands taking with them an assortment of churls and serfs to fight for their king; however, they were no match for the might of William's fighting machine, William's Army of young knights. The autumn sun caught the shields of the knights as they rode their horses down the makeshift planks from the ships.

The knights led the ranks of foot soldiers as they made their way to fight the Saxons. The deadly broadswords hanging from their waists, all of the soldiers had one single purpose in mind, to defeat Harold and place William on the throne. At the head of the columns rode William's most loyal knight, Gilbert Bayeux, along with Gunter Hinds and Rolf De-Wooley. These three knights would lay down their life for William.

They were brave and well-trained, and they rode and cut down the Saxon knights and churls from the English villagers. The churls hadn't a chance. They were more used to tilling the fields and tending the animals. The battlefield was awash with blood; the cries of the wounded and dying could be heard above the clash of steel. As Norman knights cut down the ill-prepared Saxons, none of whom had been trained in the art of fighting. The Normans had advanced a line of foot soldiers led by their superiors on horseback, the well-trained knights who represented William's fighting machine.

The Saxon thegns had left their manors and families with little or no protection at all, leaving them prey to the unscrupulous sacking and raping of the womenfolk and burning of lands by marauding Norman soldiers. These were members of the Norman army that had defected from the main army to gain riches for themselves.

King William was flanked by his loyal knights who fought at his side, loyally protecting him. Amongst the knights were Gilbert Bayeux, Rolf De-Wooley, Gunter Hinds and many more. They did not agree with the treatment the renegade soldiers meted out on peaceful villagers. The sacking and raping had not been done on William's orders. William was a fair king and wished to bring together his Norman knights and the English people as one nation. If William had caught any of his soldiers that had committed these dreadful deeds, they would have been punished severely. The three brave knights were of the same mind. Gilbert was a firm favourite of William, who admired him greatly for his brave deeds and unwavering loyalty.

William's knights were dressed in three pieces of underclothing, leggings and top leggings with fine woollen tunics and soft lawn shirts underneath. They also wore a mail coat, along with a metal helmet with a nose visor and a deadly sword hanging from their hip. The sight of a line of brave knights on horseback was impressive and intimidating to the Saxon army. Their cloaks were made of fine wool that covered their shoulders to give them warmth against the cold English weather.

These loyal knights were William's cavalry with one thought in mind, to put their Lord King William on his rightful throne. The serfs and the churls fighting had little or no protection and were quickly disposed of by the Norman knights. There were some thegns who had not sided with Harold, so they were left in peace until a knight would be gifted their lands. As their overlord, most knights respected the thegns, providing they accepted their protection, knelt and swore loyalty to the new overlord. William mostly gifted the lands that weren't prospering well or because the master was elderly or needed help. If a thegn was still young and capable of running their estate, they were left in peace.

Most of the Saxon churls and serfs thought that the Normans had been spawned by the devil and therefore worshiped the devil; suspicions were rife among the less educated. The battles raged over the English lands, and it took until 1071 to bring some sort of normality to the

English countryside. As each battle was won by the might of the Norman fighting machine, King William gifted castles and lands to his loyal knights to ensure that England continued to prosper, and life for the English people continued.

One such loyal knight was gifted the Castle Alder-Sea and lands. The knight was single-minded in making sure that England found peace after the ravages of war. He only wanted to settle in peace in England and perhaps have a family of his own. His name was Lord Gilbert Bayeux of Normandy. If the Saxons dealt fairly with him and accepted that he was the new lord, then he would deal fairly with them. However, if any of them thought that they could be lax under his rule, they would find he would rule with a hand of steel.

Packing up his waggons and entourage, he set out for the lands of Alder-sea. Looking behind at the waggons following him, he realised that his parents had been a little overzealous at packing some trifles for his solar when he arrived at the castle, and the sword he wore was his father's. He had insisted that Gilbert have it. By rights, it should have gone to one of his older brothers, but he was the unmarried one, the one who believed in William. His mother had even packed him a prie-dieu because she was afraid that he would become a heathen.

Shaking his head and smiling, he made his way ahead with a small entourage of soldiers and a couple of knights who were also loyal friends to himself. He was dressed in a dark blue tunic trimmed with fur. His leggings were a slightly paler blue, and the cloak he wore was of dark wool. He was over six foot; his eyes were a slate grey and his hair thick blonde. He had taken off his mail coat but still wore his sword on his hip.

As he rode, he wondered what welcome he would receive. He wasn't sure if there was a mistress with the thegn, or if there were any maids to become his wards. What he did know was that the sons of the manor had died in the fierce battle at the side of Harold.

Making their way across England to what would be his new home, the dust from the road was filling his mouth and nose. He held his hand up for his small band of knights and soldiers to take a break, a drink to clear their parched throats and a small rest for their mounts. They would then be sure to arrive before supper.

After all, they had taken their leave quite early the day before from William, who had promised if Matilda's lying in allowed, they would soon be visiting Gilbert who was one of his favourites. Gilbert was loyal and a fierce fighter. He would protect William at any cost. He and two knights, both Gilbert's friends, had ridden in defence of their king and fought off a band of Saxons that had him surrounded, then continued to fight at his side.

Gunter and Rolf were travelling with him to his new home before having to join William's main army an any other battles. Once more mounting his dark black destrier, he ordered his travelling companions to mount ready to move on. He preferred to continue in the daylight if they were attacked because they were Normans. They would have more chance of success in the daylight as any roaming Saxon bands would find the terrain much more familiar than they did.

Chapter 2

Meanwhile, riding back as fast as possible, Knight Godfrey was trying to gain time to Alder-Sea Castle. He was an older Saxon who was faithful to his thegn, George Roland, and wanted to warn him that a new lord was on his way. Riding into the courtyard, he was soon striding into the main hall of the manor eager to speak with his master. He bowed slightly as he came upon his master sitting in a huge chair by the fire. Spring was in the air, and it was still quite cool. George was of a good age and felt the cold these days.

'Sir, the Norman Knight Gilbert of Bayeux is on his way. What I have seen of him, sir, he appears to be fair man, firm but fair. He has been granted Castle Alder-sea and its lands by King William. He is but an hour behind me,' he said, advising his elderly master of the impending arrival of Gilbert Bayeux. 'Two other knights and a small band of soldiers are also with him.'

'I must see to the child. You watch from the bailey. Godfrey, you have done well, my old friend. You will see the dust of his horses, advise me then; from henceforth the child is to be known as my personal manservant until we can devise a plan to spirit the child away. If the child goes now, they might be spotted on the road or in the forest.'

'Aye, it will need to be a safe plan. Perhaps I myself can guide them through the forest safely, my lord, but we need to have a proper plan in place. It would be advisable to be careful and wait until the time is right.'

A quick nod of his head was all he needed to give in acknowledgement, for his Lord George was well aware that Godfrey would follow his instructions to the letter despite being tired after the long ride back to Alder-Sea.

Looking around the main hall, there were well-worn trestles with worn chairs of hewn oak lined up behind them. The rushes on the floor were changed daily and had already been scattered with sweet smelling herbs to take away the odours of daily living. Opposite the high table were a number of the same trestles and chairs to allow the important visiting neighbouring thegns to sit and converse with the lord of the manor. A huge hearth housed a roaring fire to keep the hall warm and comfortable. It indeed was a pleasant hall, Godfrey reminisced. He was always happy to return to Alder-Sea.

Godfrey followed the elderly thegn and parted as his Lord George made his way into his solar. Godfrey continued past to make his way along the dim hall. The rush bundles had not been lit yet. They would be dipped in mutton fat later and placed in the sconces to light the passageway. Right at the back, the stairs to the bailey could be seen. Walking smartly towards them, eager to do his master's bidding, he climbed upwards. He opened the trapdoor to allow him to enter the vantage point where he could watch for anyone who would be travelling to his lord's manor. They had been able to defend the Castle Alder-sea on many occasions against would be transgressors.

Here, Godfrey would patiently watch and wait, ready to warn his Lord George of any movement. Making himself comfortable on the floor, he scanned the road in front of the castle through the battlements for any sign of movement. The day was dry and the horses of anyone travelling towards them would be clearly visible as they rode towards their destination.

George Rowlands eyed the child in front of him. His heart was heavy; he must protect his grandchild from harm. He had promised his son that no harm would come to his child.

'Have you everything clear in your head? From this day forth you will be known as Guy. You must not answer to anything else. You will also have to act as a serf and not address me as anything other than master.'

'Yes,' came the short answer.

'So, henceforth this is how it will be until we can spirit you away to the nearest place of safety.'

'Yes,' the child answered again.

'I promised your father I would keep you safe and happy. I will not break my promise. You must also treat the new lord as your master. I will have to swear fealty to him as you will too. You must be on your guard at all times and must not let me down. So, your new name if asked is Guy of the Hall, you must remember to stay by my side at all times, you understand?'

'Yes, Gr- master,' the child said realising by the warning look that the elderly then gave that a mistake had nearly been made. The newly named Guy broke in, 'I'm sorry. I will remember, master, I promise. It's new to me, but I'm sure I will manage.'

'You must make sure that you do, child, or who knows what will happen to either of us.'

Turning the child around, he looked in the chest for some appropriate wear for the child. These had been supplied by a kitchen hand and had been hidden under the rest of the contents.

Seeing the look on child's face, he said, 'I know, but you cannot appear to be of noble birth. There are more ways that you could suffer other than wearing a servant's old clothes.'

'I know, master.'

'Now, behind the screen and change your clothes quickly before our new lord arrives. After all, none of us are certain what our new lord will be like.'

'Alright,' the subdued answer came. In the elderly thegn's mind was a riot of all sorts of abominations that could befall his beloved grandchild if the new lord was not as he seemed. He needed to be sure and protect him. Yes, he must think of his grandchild as him henceforth.

Passing the child lengths of linen material, he asked, 'Can you manage to bind yourself?'

'Yes and thank you, master.'

'Bring your clothes out, and I will dispose of them,' he advised.

'Yes, master,' the child replied believing the more it was said, the more he would remember. The child looked around fifteen-years-old with huge violet-blue eyes. The grandfather had cropped the golden curls on the child's head. The build was slight around five foot two. Returning from behind the screen, the child looked every inch a servant lad apart from the golden hair. It shone too much.

'We need a little grease for your hair. I'm sorry to say it's too clean for a serf,' he said.

'A little burnt mutton fat off that unlit bundle in the sconce won't smell too badly, master.'

'You hope,' the old man smiled as he regained a little of his good-natured humour.

How he wished he had the child safely away already. He selfishly had kept the child by his side not wanting to part with his only living relative. Besides, it would have been too dangerous until now with gangs of breakaway renegade Norman soldiers hiding in the woods. He needed to wait until the new lord had cleared it enough for Godfrey to move safely through the woods with the child to some abbey where the prioress would allow the child to stay. He would himself provide a dowery for its keep. The sooner Godfrey, his old friend and faithful servant, devised a plan, the sooner they would be getting the child to safety. Feeling more positive inside now he had taken the time to make the decision of removing his grandchild to safety, he turned his attention to completing the task in hand.

Reaching down the unlit bundle of rushes, he rubbed his hands through them, pleased with the result of the blackened grease upon his hands. Standing in front of the child, he began to rub the gunge into the child's golden hair making it appear dirty and not so well kept.

'I must say that looks better, and an old hat would help. Then you will really look the part.'

'Yes, master,' was the reply.

'You learn quick, my child. Make sure you keep it up.' Walking over to a chest, he rummaged through until he came to an old hat that one of his dogs had taken a fancy to. It had been chewed, but it was the ideal thing to hide the child's face a little. He then pushed the garments that the child had taken off underneath the clothing that was already in the trunk. Hopefully, anything within this solar would be left alone. He also hoped that he would be able to stay within this solar as it would suit his plans.

George Rowlands made the newly named child Guy repeat the instructions that had been given by himself to make sure that he had remembered everything they had conversed about; he was now satisfied that they could pull off the plan to keep the child's identity hidden. He intended to keep the child under his protection until they could be spirited away to a safe haven.

He himself needed to be careful how he addressed his grandchild, wishing only that life was as it had been a few years ago, peaceful and happy, and his two strong sons at his side to help him. The new lord could look at the child as an enemy and use his grandchild to cement his place as master of this manor. The thegn could not stand the thought of that. Godfrey had assured him that Gilbert Bayeux was a reasonable man. He couldn't be sure that Godfrey was right, and he preferred to err on the cautious side. If he was to believe that he was the last of the family, then Lord Gilbert would not consider him too much of a threat. He himself was thinking his time was short, and he would rest in peace if he knew the child had been taken to safety, as priories were sacred in this country.

There was a scratching heard at the door, 'Come,' the thegn called out.

Godfrey entered. 'They are nearly here, my lord.'

'Good,' came his master's answer.

Godfrey was amazed at the transformation of the child. Looking towards the boy, he said in amazement, 'By the holy saints, I swear I wouldn't have known yon child if we had met in one of the corridors.'

The newly named Guy kept his eyes downcast and kept his place as he had been told. The child's heart was heavy at the thought of leaving his beloved grandfather. He had to believe he was Guy now and not think of the other identity. He was afraid that the carefree days of childhood were gone. He felt that the new identity had placed a heavy burden on all three of them. His parents were already dead and buried, and he had only just come to terms with that. Thinking 'twas hard, yes, 'twas hard, and he knew Grandfather would be hurting inside too. They would only then have memories of each other. Guy was also aware that his grandfather was now frail, and it could soon be the time to leave him when he was the only relative in the world he had left. Not daring to shed the tears felt behind the violet blue eyes, Guy was aware that

Grandfather would be greatly distressed at this, so for his sake, he must control himself. And he must give a good account of a serf. He, Guy as he was to be known, must be brave and not gentle; he must be subservient and not act above the station of a serf; he also needed to ensure that as Guy a young serf not to let Grandfather down to ensure his safety as well. All these rules were new to him but with the determination of the young, he swore not to let him down.

Unsure of what the new lord would be like, that was the only worry that went through his head. He looked the part, he now needed to act the part. All that Guy wanted was for the Normans to treat his grandfather with kindness and courtesy, hoping and praying that would be the case. If they did, it wouldn't matter about him, but his grandfather was getting frail and weak. He should not have to bear this burden at this time of life when he was sick and ailing; however, war did not consider people who did not wish for it. The elderly thegn only wished for peace but not all Saxons did. There were some only too willing to take up arms again.

'Would you like a drink, master?' he asked, determined to take on the role.

'Yes, Guy, you can quickly go to the kitchens and advise cook of the new lord's arrival and bring me a flagon of wine with three extra goblets. Make sure you return at once. I need you with me. I will not shame us, Godfrey, and I can have the wine ready to quench the new lord's thirst after the dust from the ground.'

'Yes, master,' came the young serf's answer. The slight figure left the solar and quickly make haste to the kitchens.

Once there, he passed the message on to cook and the scullery maid. 'Pray, tell me, how are you to be known?' young Enid asked.

'Guy of the Hall.'

'Oh, that's easy. It's what we call you now, a shortened version of your birth name, yes, Guy.'

'Yes,' Guy smiled back at Enid. They had been firm friends and playmates when small, as class had no part in children's lives and games.

'I'll carry it back for you, Guy.'

'No, I need to do this myself. I have to blend in, and I'm certain I can carry this off. After all, I've spent enough time with you.'

'By the holy saints, you have,' she said laughing back at him. Guy took the tray she offered and quickly made his way back through the main hall to find his grandfather already in there with Godfrey awaiting his return.

George sat on a chair and by the side of it was a small stool, 'Put it on here, boy, and sit at my side and only speak when you are addressed by your masters. Is that clear?'

'Yes, master,' came the short answer. Godfrey took another chair nearby as they listened to the clip clop of horses as the new lord and his entourage entered the outer courtyard.

Dismounting and walking towards the stables across the courtyard, a groom came out and took the horses' reins, bowing his head slightly to the knights, not knowing how to act. He, Aldric, was just a servant. He would leave it to his lord's own knights to look towards the safety of the castle, and he would take care of the horses, that was his task. Although he didn't feel too kindly disposed to waiting on Normans, now it looked as if they would be his masters. Inside his heart, Lord George would always be his master. Come what may, he would follow his orders. As a small lad, he had been treated kindly by his master, and he had never spoken harshly to him. He was comfortable working here at Alder-Sea, but now he was unsure of what his life would be like.

Muffled footsteps were heard as the three knights followed by a couple of soldiers entered the main hall. The elderly thegn motioned the young Guy to stand and help him rise as he had already been told to do. George's voice rang out clearly as he addressed the young knight in blue.

'Welcome, my lord, to your new manor. Guy, pour some refreshment for your new lord to wash away the dust from their throats, but first water from the jug for them to wash their hands,' he said gesturing to the rough copper bowel on a stand.

Guy walked over to the jug and emptied some water into the bowl, picking up some clean fabric for the young men to dry their hands on. Guy retreated quickly as he looked up and grey eyes met the lavender blue. Had he seen something? the newly named Guy thought as the knight gave a searching look in his direction. Quickly, he moved to fill the wooden goblets with wine, at the same time ensuring that he didn't spill any causing his new master to cuff his ears. He didn't know how his grandfather would respond if he did. He offered the new master the first goblet and kept his eyes averted as he did so.

Looking at the boy, the new lord said, 'Pray, don't be afraid, boy, I'm not the devil, and I'm sure I'm not hungry enough to eat you right now.' This brought an outburst of laughter from the other two knights at Gilbert's jest to make the elderly thegn feel more at ease.

Quickly seizing advantage of the new lord's jest, George said, 'This is my faithful companion, Godfrey, and my personal serf, Guy, who helps me through the day with personal needs and attire, my lord. I only ask of you to allow me to continue my friendship with Godfrey and for me to keep Guy as he knows my needs of washing and dressing. I need a little help these days, my lord. Age has no respect for the body,' George said with a slight bow of the head.

'Sir, I am the new master of these lands and Castle Alder-sea; however, you will be under my protection, you and any other issue of your family. Are there no mistress or maidens here belonging you?'

'Nay, none. My sons believed in Harold's cause, so they followed their belief. Myself, I chose rightly or wrongly to stay and look after what were then my lands and the villager serfs and churls alike. Their safety was my responsibility. I surrender them to you the victors and await your decision.'

'Sir, I will not demean you so. You will, however, remain under my protection. I would treat you no different than my own father. As for your friendship with Godfrey, why would I not allow you your old friend? I also value my friends. As you see, my good friends Rolf and Gunter, we will all be old friends at some point in our lives.'

'It is good to see that you too value friendship and understand the importance of it,' George replied.

'One thing I cannot understand, sir, is why you have picked a boy so puny to attend to your needs when there are many here much stronger. The lad is pale and pretty, yes pretty is the word?' he said as he rubbed his chin thoughtfully. 'Perhaps we could find him a less demanding position and ensure you have someone young but strong to help you with your daily tasks.'

'I prefer to continue with Guy's help, sir. He looks puny, but he is strong enough to fit my needs. I have him well trained, and he sleeps on a pallet in my room so that he is always on hand. I would ask you, sir, if you could make it known that he is not to be hurt or belittled by his size, some of your soldiers could see him as an object of fun,' the thegn answered as red flags rose in his mind at the knight using pretty to describe Guy.

'They already are aware that all at Alder-sea are under my protection and that I am now master here. They are not to mete out any punishment here without bringing the crime to me, does that satisfy you, sir?'

George bowed his head in acknowledgement. 'Do you wish that myself and the serf move to one of the outer shelters in the grounds?'

'No, I don't I wish you to, you need to stay here in the warmth of the castle,' he said this as he looked at the elderly thegn's weather-beaten face and the deep furrows of age. Sadly, one day they would all come to this stage in their life if they were lucky enough.

Gilbert had one wish in mind and that was to unite England in the name of his new King William. He wished for peace. He was aware though that if William charged him to take up arms against any of the small pockets of Saxons that kept the rebellion up, he would have no alternative than to take up his arms again in his king's name to quell the fighting.

At this moment in time, he hoped that it would not be the case. He wished to catch his breath for a while and rest whilst seeing to the affairs here. He was sure that the George Rowlands would help him understand all the areas that he needed to understand and help him identify problems in one way or another. They needed each other to make this new life work. Besides, George Rowlands needed a strong person beside him. It must have hurt losing his two sons in the ravages of a war that no one had cared for.

He also saw that there was plenty to put right in the fields. Some of the harvest had rotted before it had been gathered. Mainly because the churl that had been granted the land to farm, had followed Harold into battle and perished in doing so. He needed to look at the serfs applying to farm the strips of land and choose new people to farm them. Also, he needed to see that the stores would be fully stocked for the cold winters ahead. William had given him free warrant to hunt in the forest, so once he had checked the stores for what they needed, he would dispatch soldiers to hunt for deer and wild boar. Spring would soon move into summer; however, the seasons went quickly. They would always have to plan in advance and be ready for what could be a harsh winter in the inclement weather, thus, making sure no man or maid went hungry.

'Now, sir, to business. I need to know how many solars do we have in this castle of ours?' he asked including the thegn in his ownership to show he meant him no harm.

'We have two large solars off this main hall, and a further three off the corridor not quite as large, as well as a small one higher up just under the bailey.'

'So, if William decides to visit, we have a large solar we can accommodate him in for his use.' William could sometimes just turn up to get to know his subjects and again if they dealt fairly with William. William was sure to treat them fairly, he thought. Looking around the banqueting hall, he thought it was light and airy with ample trestles and seating.

At the moment, he would not mix Normans and Saxons together with ale. He knew better than that. He would save that for another day. They would deal better with each other once they had time to forge allegiances. He would, however, choose a Saxon reeve for the castle to bring the Saxons and the Normans together to work side by side to show they would be all treated the same, man, maid and child. He would also need to discuss tithes and deeds with the elderly thegn to make sure that the villagers who had been granted a portion of land to farm were making full use of the facilities to grow a good harvest and raise animals. Also, that they could provide the Castle Alder-sea with taxes to help the villagers who were struggling. He would see that no family in his village suffered poverty providing they were or had been good workers.

'Now, sir, do you reside in one of the solars off the main hall?' Gilbert asked.

'Yes, I do, sir, but if you wish myself and my serf to move to one of the outer buildings or to a smaller solar, I will do so.' George of Alder-sea awaited his new master's answer with bated breath. He didn't wish to change his solar, as it would make things much harder for Guy to reach the meeting point with Godfrey to smuggle the child away.

'There will be no need for that, sir, if you show me to the second one. I presume that is empty?'

'It is, my lord,' George answered, as Guy quickly came to the thegn's aid as he struggled to stand. With his hand on the shoulder of Guy, he led Gilbert and his knights to a corridor off the main solar. The empty solar was bare, there was not even a bed or a pallet in there, so, for once, Gilbert gave thanks for his mother's fussiness in filling his wagon with comforts for him.

Turning to George, Gilbert said, "Perhaps you would like to rest before supper. Your serf, Guy, can give you his arm and bring you to your seat at my side, sir, and after supper, one of my knights will guide you back. Guy can take a bite to eat back with him and be ready to assist you on your return.'

'I thank you, my lord, and I am a little weary now. A rest would be a comfort.' Looking at him, Gilbert realised that indeed the thegn was weary. Looking at the watery, red-rimmed eyes and the thin frame, it would be a wonder if he would see the winter out. Gilbert thought if that was so, he would do his best to make his last days a comfort. And yes, the garments he wore were of good thread, but they hung on his wasting frame. William had been right when he said that reports led him to understand that the thegn residing at Alder-sea was old and ailing and needed a strong overlord to make the villagers more successful to bring in the taxes. This way they could rebuild England after the ravages of war.

With a wry smile, he thought the villagers would think that the Normans only thought of money, but not so. Taxes were to aid all of the villagers. It would be for their benefit because they collected taxes to help the poor and needy to survive. One of the areas he would check would be if all of the strips of land were being worked and the churls were making the most of the harvesting and that the tally of grain along with other crops were providing sufficient funds in the form of tax to the manor's coffers. This would keep the manor and the village in good repair. And food stores would be full enough to feed all throughout the winter months, along with stocks of wood to keep their fires burning bright and warm.

'I can manage now, sir. You take your rest, and I'm sure you will enjoy your supper tonight and be better for it.'

Turning to his knights, he said, 'You, Gunter, take a soldier and find the kitchens and make sure we have enough food to feed Normans and Saxons alike at supper, and leave the pretty maids alone for the moment, my good friend,' with a laugh.

Turning to Rolf, he said, 'You and I can supervise my belongings from the wagons. We will need a couple of serfs to help transform that cold empty solar.'

So, marching outside, the mighty Norman machinery was soon put into action. It wasn't long before a bed had been erected with a straw mattress and flaxen sheets covering it, along with a bearskin for warmth. Tapestries were hung on the walls and floors swept with fresh rushes scented with herbs laid down on the floor. Two large floor standing candlesticks stood either side of the fireplace; the sconces held rush bundles freshly dipped in mutton fat ready to light up. Placed in the corner was the prie-dieu that his mother had insisted he would need, a roughly hewn wooden chair complete with tapestry cushion that his sisters had provided. The solar looked fit for habitation now. The fire opening now had a fire with the flames flickering on the walls and giving warmth to the chamber.

'Well, Rolf, it looks fit for the master of the manor. You and Gunter can take your pick of the other solars for now, and if we have visitors, we can move our sleeping quarters around to accommodate them, for William is sure to visit this area in the future.'

'He could, but it depends on the needs of Queen Matilda. She is with child and near to lying in so it depends on the queen,' answered Rolf with a smile.

'Yes, you are right on that score. William will see that Matilda is cared for above all else.

'Now all I need is to have a couple of serfs to bring in a bath and have it filled with hot water, and then we may wash away the dust we have gathered on our clothes with the long ride.'

Soon, Gilbert was lying in a bath of scented water. It had been days since any of them had been able to take a bath. As he lay there, his mind turned to Guy. He somewhat intrigued him. The first thing he had noticed had been his large violet blue eyes, and his slender grace. His clothes needed to be changed if he was to stay in the castle with them. It would keep a couple of days, he thought. The thegn had endured enough for the day. He had surrendered his lands with good grace and strength, and it couldn't have been easy. So, he would attend to the young Guy's cleanliness on another occasion once the old man was aware that he, Gilbert Bayeux, meant them no harm. He just wanted Norman and Saxon to thrive side by side in this fair land.

Finding some clean clothes, he once more felt refreshed. Calling Rolf in he said, 'The bath is all yours and Gunter's. You need to send for the serfs to empty it and supply you with fresh water. I will now have a walk around my castle and speak to the churls and serfs.'

'Well, you will be well advised to take someone with you, Gilbert. You are unknown to these Saxons, yet.' Gilbert just smiled and strapped his sword to his waist and tapped it, striding out into the main hall where he found Godfrey standing.

'Perhaps you would like my company, my lord,' he offered.

'That would be most welcome, Godfrey,' he answered, strolling out into the sunshine with Godfrey at his side. As he moved amongst the village churls, he noticed another young boy not yet grown enough to fight or to till the fields, realising he would need a page himself to take on tasks of running messages. He could not use his knights for such menial work.

'What's your name, boy?' he asked.

'Wulf,' came his clear answer looking proudly into his new lord's eyes. He had dark brown hair and green eyes flecked with grey. He wasn't pretty like Guy, but he would fit the bill.

Godfrey broke in saying, 'Wulf's father died in the battles alongside the young masters. He has to do what work he can to support his mother, sir.'

'Well, Wulf, you can present yourself at the manor with your mother. You will be trained as a page, and your mother can be put to work in the kitchens. Make a note, Godfrey, that two sets of clothes each must be made. Two for Wulf and two for Guy so they can be recognised as part of the manor staff and must not be apprehended or hurt in any way. The threads that Guy wears are not fitting for residing in the castle. I like pages and serfs to be clean and presentable.'

'Yes, my lord, I agree with you. It will make them easily recognisable.'

Chapter 3

Gilbert and Godfrey spent a pleasant couple of hours
walking around and speaking to the villagers that were to
be his responsibility. They would answer to him and also
be protected by him. If there were any disputes to solve, he
would be the one to oversee and pass judgement; so, he
needed to get the feel of who was who and of course, the
ones he had to watch and keep in line. There were free
men and tied men, and he would need to work out the
identities of each family. With the help of the thegn and
Godfrey, he would perhaps be well-prepared for the day
that they would have to kneel at his feet and swear fealty
to him as their lord and master. Gilbert rubbed his chin. He
needed to have the ceremony arranged swiftly, that way he
would be able to recognise by the Saxons' demeaner, who
would blend into the new life and who would need to be
kept in line.

The one person that he had doubts about was the surly
blacksmith who was a free man. He would have the option
of swearing fealty to him or leaving the castle, and he
would not be allowed to work for a year and would not be
allowed to come back to this estate again. Gilbert noticed
that there was a certain strength of character in this man,
and he felt that once he was on your side that he would be
loyal and fight his corner and, more important, firm and
fair to Normans and Saxons alike. As he was taking speech
with him, he was forming an idea in his head, but once
more, he needed to have speech with the thegn and
Godfrey to run his ideas past them. After all, they were
better acquainted with him and would be more aware if his
opinions of the blacksmith matched with theirs.

'Come, Godfrey, we need some refreshment to quench our thirst before suppertime.'

'That would be most agreeable, my lord,' he answered, as they walked side by side making their way back to the castle.

Walking into the main hall, Gilbert accosted Guy walking through the room with a tray and a flagon of wine set upon it.

'Is that for your master, Guy?'

'Yes, my lord,' Guy answered.

'Well, make haste and instruct your master that if he is rested enough, perhaps he would like to join us to quench his thirst and to have speech. Place the wine on the table, there appears to be fresh goblets there already and some wine.'

'Yes, my lord. My master asked me to have Enid bring it in for your return, so I brought it through myself as they were so busy in the kitchens, and then I'm to return and help my master to ready himself for supper, my lord.'

Gilbert watched the slight figure walk towards the corridor which held the thegn's solar, his brows drawn together. Why did he feel drawn to the graceful boy with the beautiful lavender blue eyes? Shaking himself he thought, *it has been too long since you had a fair maiden, my man, pull yourself together.*

Walking over to the roughly hewn table, he poured himself and Godfrey a generous goblet of wine. 'Your good health, Godfrey and to the alliance of Saxons and Normans alike. May we learn to live side by side in peace.'

'Good health to you, my lord. I feel the country has had enough of war. We do need to build and grow England in peace, sir.'

'Aye, you are right, Godfrey, peace is what we need to heal our people. If we pull together, Saxons and Normans side by side, we could build a strong and successful manor and village for all to enjoy.'

At that moment, George walked in, his hand resting on Guy's shoulder.

'Are you rested, sir?' Godfrey asked his master refraining from calling him my lord or master, as he was well aware that was Gilbert's status now.

'Yes, thank you both. I feel much better. Sometimes I forget my age, a lesson I must heed.'

'Come sit, George, and partake of some wine. Guy, wine for your master,' Gilbert instructed. Guy immediately filled a goblet of wine, offering it to the thegn who took it with a nod of his head. Guy bowed slightly and backed away to stand by the door awaiting further instructions as he had seen his grandfather's serfs do. As he stood there, he remembered suppers over the years with his father and uncles along with neighbouring thegns, eating and drinking, sometimes joking and even having good natured arguments. That was before war tore through England killing family and friends alike and for what, he thought, power and money.

'I have asked Godfrey to order two outfits of good thread for Guy and my new page, Wulf, befitting their status in the manor. This will make them more recognisable as staff belonging to the manor, and it will allow them to walk around the village without being accosted.'

'That is most generous, my lord,' George answered.

'You can call me Gilbert; it will be more fitting, George. You and I are of equal status as is Godfrey. We need to work together and show a united front.'

George bowed slightly, his mind skipping ahead to Guy. He needed to be present to protect the child when he was fitted with new clothes.

'Did you have a pleasant passage amongst your villagers?' Gilbert the thegn asked.

'Enlightening, George. You have most of the villagers farming their strips of land effectively, and come spring, there will be a good crop. We do need to build a few more shelters ready for visitors who may visit. I will need you to show me the best area we could manage this without disrupting any land that is needed for extending farmland. We will put aside time for tomorrow to do this.'

'There is the land behind the dovecote, sir. You were looking at it wondering how to improve that area,' Godfrey reminded the thegn.

'Yes, Godfrey, that would indeed improve that area if Gilbert is agreeable,' came his answer.

'I have decided that I will not mix Saxon and Norman at supper when they are drinking ale tonight, George. What are your thoughts on my decision?'

'We will have to sometime, Gilbert, as they will need to come to terms with working together as one nation.'

'You are right of course, George, but if we can find time to go over the tithes and bond people of the manor, we could arrange a feast for Saturday. That will be the day for the villagers to swear fealty to me as their new overlord.'

At this point, Godfrey said, 'That would be a very good plan. Everyone is more amenable when their belly is full and they have imbibed a little ale, a good way to bring the Saxons and Normans together as one.'

'Yes, to celebrate a new era in their life would be a good idea,' George added.

'Right, Guy, would you like to check how the kitchens are getting on with tonight's banquet? Then you can wait for your master's instructions to refresh himself before supper and delivering him back to eat.'

Guy slipped off to the kitchen to check on supper and noticed that nothing had been spared. There were pies and roasts galore; whole pigs had been roasted and birds cooked to perfection; kitchen hands were preparing to carry trenchers into the large dining hall along with wooden goblets.

Guy remembered the rare glass goblets that belonged to his grandmother that would have been used to sup wine at any feast given for neighbouring thegns and family when they had dined with her grandparents and his mother and father. A tear appeared in the corner of his eye as he thought of days past only to be hurriedly wiped away as anger rose in the child's throat.

'Will you be dining in the hall, Guy?' asked Enid.

'No, I'm to dine alone and one of Gilbert's knights will guide my master back,' careful not to say grandfather afraid that someone might hear, or that he would let grandfather down.

'I'll see to your supper, Guy, and bring it to you,' Enid said with a smile.

'Thank you, that will be very agreeable, Enid,' was the answer as he returned to report to Gilbert. 'I have done your bidding my lord, and supper will soon be served.'

'Have you arranged your food, Guy?'

'Yes, my lord, Enid was kind enough to ask me about my supper.'

'Good,' came Gilbert's reply as he turned his attention to Rolf and Gunter as they entered the main hall to join their friend.

Soon the voices of the Norman soldiers were heard as they walked in to join their lord for supper. It sounded as if some of them had already imbibed their fair share of ale.

Gilbert offered his arm to George and assisted him to his place at the high table next to him on his right. Sitting next to him were Rolf and Gunter. Godfrey was also placed at the high table on the left of Gilbert.

He chose to do this to show that the elderly thegn remained under his protection and was still of good standing at the castle. Gilbert knew that the knights that had travelled with him would understand without being reminded. His soldiers, he was not quite sure. They were effective fighters and would be alert on guard. Some would be on the make, and he needed to be sure he was aware of anything afoot that he did not approve of. Mostly they were loyal to him. The odd soldier needed to be watched, so he needed them to be aware that George Rowlands was to be treated with respect.

Soon the hall was full of Norman soldiers who were full of good-natured banter as they jockeyed for the different dishes that had been prepared by Wally, the head cook for the castle.

Slowly, the main hall began to empty as most of the Norman soldiers began to feel the urge to visit the outside privy after imbibing so much ale with their meal or to take their positions upon guard, or the lucky ones went to their allotted quarters to catch some much-needed sleep. It had been a long journey for all of them. It had also been very tiring for all of them, including their Lord Gilbert. Rolf kindly escorted George back to his solar and bid him a goodnight.

Gilbert lingered on the main hall, his mind going over the frailty of the elderly thegn. He had looked more than tired tonight even though he had rested most of the afternoon.

If they could agree on the land by the dovecotes to build extra shelters, then he would spend a day going through the tithes and bonds of the serfs that had been granted land to work on. Then once he had knowledge of each and every churl or serf that worked on the land and the state of the taxes paid, he was sure he would have a firm grasp on the income for the castle and the people it had to support.

Gilbert's mind once more wandered to Guy. The lad seemed genuinely attached to his master, and he was certain that the elderly thegn would not be with them for long. He also realised that Guy needed to be protected once this happened, and he mentally made up his mind when the time came to take the lad as an extra page in his household. Perhaps with a little training and more food, he would become more manly and brawny, but of course, he could not quite see this. The lad, as well as being slight and puny, was incredibly graceful, and this intrigued him. Never before had he seen a boy with these attributes. Usually if they were puny, they would be ailing in one way or another, and Gilbert could not see any trace of disease attached to the child. After all, if the boy was ailing, it would show in one way or another.

Having a last walk around the perimeters of the castle to check the soldiers on watch were ample for the castle's protection, and after saying a last goodnight to Rolf and Gunter, he made his way to his solar. All appeared to be well. It was time for him to retire to his solar. He made a striking figure as he strolled back through the main hall towards the passage to retire.

Sitting in the one chair by the fire, he went over his plans for tomorrow. He needed to be precise in his decisions. He didn't want William to regret granting him the lands and manor and placing the lives of the inhabitants in his hands. He already realised that they needed to be a safe pair of hands. Thinking once more of his family back in Normandy, he began to remove his clothes. Once this was done, he snuffed out the lights in the scones. Climbing into bed and pulling the bearskin up under his chin, it wasn't long before he slept. The journey over the last few days had been long and tiring. He was a little weary and needed time to recharge his energy.

Chapter 4

Morning came and Gilbert sat in his main hall before a roaring fire. Enid had just brought him bread, ham and a flagon of ale to break his fast.

'Have you seen to George and Guy's food yet?' He was still concerned about the thegn.

'Yes, my lord, I have sent Roland the kitchen boy to serve them.'

'Good, I will give them time and go and bid them good morning.' Enid curtseyed and quickly left the main hall making her way to George's solar. Scratching the door, she waited for her master to bid her to come in. Enid quickly passed on the fact that Gilbert would shortly be following her, warning George and Guy to be dressed for his visit.

'Thank you, Enid. I will now be aware that we could have visitors at any time and thus must make sure we are always prepared.'

'I will make sure I rise early, master, and make sure I'm always ready before he has time to visit our solar.'

'And I, Guy, must find out how safe the forest is. We must put our plans in place. Time is going quickly,' the thegn said with a serious look on his face. In his heart of hearts, he realised that he wouldn't be for this earth long. He, George Rowlands, knew he would soon be meeting his maker, and his grandchild would not have his protection. Godfrey would have to check if it was safe to put their plan into action. They must remove the child out of harm's way.

Soon Gilbert was at the door, and as he entered, he noticed that both George and Guy were dressed and had broken their fast. Guy was busy putting the remains of their bread and drinks on a tray to remove back to the kitchens.

'Are you feeling rested, George? If you are, I would appreciate an hour of your time to look at the land by the dovecotes,' Gilbert said with a smile.

George bowed slightly, saying, 'Of course, my lord, I am at your disposal.'

'We will instruct Enid to collect the remains of your meal, and Guy can accompany us; we might have need of him. Then you can make me familiar with the tithes and the bond men on the land.'

'Of course, my lord, I will be happy to pass the work of managing the papers for this manor. Sometimes it can be quite a headache. It's a young man's task, and my brain no longer has the concentration.'

'I'm sure with your help I might be able to come to grips with it, but I too might end up with a headache,' he jokingly said.

The small group left to make their way to the dovecotes. Gilbert surveyed the land. There was a small garden in front with a selection of herbs growing.

Guy, without thinking, said, 'We need to keep this patch of herbs to sweeten the fresh rushes we put on the floor.' Gilbert gave him a sharp look at his input.

'Guy knows I like the rushes we put down fresh to have sweet smelling herbs from the garden. It's just a little job he does.'

'I see,' Gilbert said once more giving Guy a searching look. Guy realised that he should not have involved himself in giving counsel of what should or shouldn't be done. He was now just a serf. He could have bitten his tongue off making such a mistake. He must make sure it didn't happen again. He hoped Grandfather wouldn't be angry with him.

George began to speak again, 'The land behind the dovecote would make an excellent stretch to erect more dwellings for visitors. You could even add another privy to accommodate the extra guests.'

'Yes, this will do well, George. We can make our way back to Rolf and Gunter. They can put some men to work. It's better to be prepared and not have to do it in a hurry. Come, let's go back and instruct that the work be started. I'll wager you will be ready to sit down and have a drink before we look at anything else.'

Later, they were sitting in a small room used to hold court and to deal with the complaints of the churls who worked the land, as well as receive the taxes from the harvests of the strips of land that had been granted to different churls or serfs. Gilbert was busy checking that the strips of land were being farmed at a profit and checking who was who on each strip of land.

'As you see, Gilbert, they are all up to date. The gathering of taxes is done every quarter, so they have another three months to trade before they are due.'

'Yes, you have kept them extremely well, and my work has been made easy by your help and co-operation.'

At that point, Gunter and Rolf entered, 'Good morning, Gilbert. It is a fine morning for hunting so with your permission, we will take a few soldiers and make sure the forest is not full of villains and renegades, Saxon or Normans alike. We need the forest to be clear and to give safe passage through for visitors.'

'Excellent idea. At the same time, you could perhaps manage a little hunting to help keep our stores full. Before you go, you can set a detail of soldiers to begin the erection of dwellings behind the dovecote. It's an ideal piece of land.'

'We will do just that, sir,' Rolf answered. 'Right, Gunter, let's get to before we visit the forest and search out either food or men, either will do.' They pushed each other in jest as they left the main hall.

Gilbert looked at Godfrey as he joined them in the room. 'I'm glad that you have joined us, Godfrey. I've had an idea that I must run past both of you. Yesterday when I walked with you, Godfrey, we came upon the blacksmith, Percival Long. We need a strong reeve for the castle, and he appears to be loyal and strong, just what we need. How say you two?'

'Would it work?!' Godfrey exclaimed.

'And you, George?' Gilbert asked.

'It could work well to bring the Saxons and Normans together. He is a just man; you have some innovated ideas, Gilbert. This is something that I might not have thought about, but I can see the merit in it, yes, I can,' George answered truthfully thinking the new Lord Gilbert was a shrewd man.

'Then that is what we'll do. He will be told on Saturday when everyone will need to swear fealty to me. That will be his test.' Both men nodded their heads in agreement.

'Now a drink, Godfrey. I'll leave you with George and Guy, and I will check that Rolf and Gunter have followed my instructions to start work on our dwellings behind the dovecote. Make sure you rest before supper.' The last remark was aimed at George.

'I will, Gilbert,' the old thegn answered as Gilbert made to leave the meeting.

'Come, Godfrey, take me back to my solar, and you, Guy, can fetch some ale from that rogue Wally who runs the kitchens.' Putting his hand on Guy's shoulder, they made their way to the solar.

Guy left to carry his message. He would also dally and have a chat with Enid whilst there. This would give George time to speak with Godfrey before Guy returned. It was important that Godfrey and himself sorted a plan before he left this mortal coil. He needed to ensure his grandchild's safety as soon as possible.

Looking at Godfrey, he silently motioned for him to close the door. 'We must make haste and form a plan; I feel my time is short. The child must be taken to safety before he is forced to grieve for me,' said George.

'You can't be sure, my lord, how long you will be with us, but it is prudent for us to check if we can successfully implement a plan to get the child away to the Holy Mother at the priory.'

'I know, Godfrey, but we must be ready, and if we make plans, we can move quickly if necessary.'

'If we wait for a month to pass, my lord, that will give us some idea of the safety of the forest.'

'Yes, once we are aware how things stand, Godfrey, we can start to make sure that Guy is aware what we have in mind.'

'It will be easy to get the child away from the castle through the secret passage into the dell,' Godfrey answered.

'Once there, he must wait for you to join him as soon as possible. Once you can get to him, I'm sure you both will have safe passage if you keep to the dense part of the trees,' George said to Godfrey.

'It's not unusual for me to ride alone early to check the castle grounds and yes, patience is the key here. We won't make Guy aware until the last minute. We don't want any tears or tantrums from the child,' Godfrey counselled.

'Of course, my lord, put yourself in the child's shoes. He loves you, and you are all the family the child has. It is sure to hurt him. We need to be careful how we tell him.'

'I too will hurt, Godfrey. The child is all I have left of my family, and I don't intend that the child be used. Trust me, Godfrey, I'm sure it will be better for the child in the priory than looking over his shoulder here.'

At that moment, someone scratched on the door, and Guy entered with a flagon of ale for his grandfather and his old friend. Guy was well aware that they had sent him on an errand to enable the two men to talk. He also knew that the words spoken would be about him and that it made his heart heavy to think that he might soon be parted from his beloved grandfather. Looking around at the familiar chamber, usually he would only be in this solar to converse with the elderly man. Instructions had been to empty the solar that Guy had used completely so there would be no sign of family left, and as it was, there was not a shred visible of anyone using that particular solar.

If asked, he would explain that once the thegn had been aware of his sons' demise, he did not want a reminder of them left to upset him. They were, after all, his sons, and he had loved them. Gilbert reminded him of his sons in lots of ways, the same proud strength and bearing of the nobility. George was finding himself liking Gilbert, and he had expected himself not to.

Walking to the small table that held some goblets, Guy silently poured the two old friends a drink, whilst asking, 'May I also take a small goblet, sir?'

'You may, Guy.' So, pouring a small goblet, he walked to his pallet and sat quietly there.

'Gunter has soldiers in the forest cutting and transporting wood to complete some shelters. Looking how quickly they are working, we will soon have a lot more outside solars for visitors, my lord.'

'Yes, the Norman machinery works fast, my old friend,' George answered as he watched the emotion flash across Guy's face, fully aware that Guy knew that something was afoot.

George sighed and said, 'I think I'll take a little rest now, Godfrey, if you'll help me onto the bed.' Godfrey helped him up and assisted him lying down, covering him with the bearskin for warmth. He bid Guy to watch over him.

'I will, sir,' came his answer as Godfrey left them alone. Guy's heart was heavy with sadness as he watched his elderly grandfather. His breathing was shallow, and it was obvious that he was weary. All Guy wished for was to stay and look after him until the end. He knew that he would have to obey his grandfather and that was to leave when the time was ready. He would no longer be here in the home he held dear but amongst strangers without his beloved grandfather. It meant that if their plan was successful, Guy would be likely never talk with his grandfather ever again. His heart was heavy with grief, and he was finding it hard to come to terms with the thought. Did Grandfather not understand he was his world and he loved him so?

Guy sat quietly not daring to keep himself occupied with his usual tasks. Sitting quietly was the only respite from boredom in case anyone found him doing inappropriate tasks for a young man.

Guy sat there most of the day. It was getting late when Godfrey returned to remind them that supper would be in half an hour. So, Godfrey gently shook his master to wake him.

'Come, George, supper will soon be ready, and Gilbert is incorporating a few of the Saxon elders mixed in with the Normans to integrate them slowly. He expects you to sup with him.'

'Aye, Godfrey, I'll soon be up and ready, my friend,' he answered. Guy quickly stood and made sure his lord had water to wash with and helped him to change his tunic, adding a cloak for him to wear as this time of the year was sometimes cold in the main hall.

Striding out flanked by Godfrey and Guy, he sat himself at the head table at the side of Gilbert. Talk between the five men turned to the upcoming celebrations for Saturday, and of course, the building of the new dwellings. Guy noticed that Gilbert was watching him intently as he walked away. He had not meant to look, but it might have been that Guy himself had taken in the broad physique of Gilbert and his almost white blond hair that shone like spun gold in the light of the sconces, and what appeared to him his great height as he looked down from the top table onto the seated Saxons and Normans readying himself for any arguments. On the whole, the seated soldiers and Saxon elders appeared to be integrating well. Gilbert was well pleased with the decision he had made.

Years ago, Guy and his friends had played games deep in the forest of knights and damsels in distress. He could see Gilbert as one of the knights that had rescued the damsels and carried them off. Enid and a couple of the serfs' young sons played the game. There were also caves deep in the wood, but they had been forbidden to wander that far in the forest and to stay near to the edge of the castle. He was ashamed to say that they hadn't always obeyed their elders, resulting in having their ears cuffed when they were found out.

Walking back to the solar, Guy found Enid there already with a good portion of bread, meat, and fruit, and a draft of ale. There was already wine standing on the table if he required it. Guy was by now quite hungry, although he didn't usually eat a great deal. He was now doing menial work, not that much, but enough for him eat a little more. Enid dawdled a little, laughing over their escapades when they were younger, and Guy said Gilbert put him in mind of the knights they would make up as children.

'You like him then?' Enid asked which made Guy go red.

'He seems quite fair, and he treats my lord well,' he replied non-committedly.

'Aye, he appears to ask and not order, and a lot of the villagers were afraid of him,' Enid replied.'

'I do think he is as handsome as any knight we imagined in our childhood games, even if he is a Norman,' Guy answered quietly.

Enid placed her hand across her mouth. 'You like him!' she whispered.

'I do. It might be because he has been kind to my master. Aye, I do like him,' came his hushed confession.'

'Is it only because of the kindness of our new lord?' Enid queried.

'I don't know. I just like him, and 'tis wrong of me. He is a Norman, and as such, they are our enemies. I'm sure our master would not approve, although they do have good speech together.'

'I think that perhaps it is to bring peace to the manor and to keep us safe from war,' Enid replied.

'Aye. I suppose, he is our enemy though, and as such, I shouldn't like him. It is confusing. When I look at him, I must be a little frightened, as it makes my stomach flutter,' came Guy's answer.

'He does appear to be a good enemy, and some of our people are still afeared of him,' came Enid's answer.

'Methinks that could change once they get used to him. It hasn't taken me long to like him, has it now,' Guy replied.

'I'll see you in the morning," Enid said, "Make sure you don't let our master George aware of your likes. He could be angry with you, and we don't want that, do we?'

'Yes, of course, and you had better return to the kitchens or you'll have Wally after you. He can be quite harsh if you are not back to help serve the main hall. It would mean it could be late when he gets to eat.'

'Aye, I'm off,' she replied and disappeared through the door, flying down the corridor to the kitchens, hoping that Wally had not noticed her prolonged absence.

Guy sat quietly eating his supper waiting for his master to return. The solar was warm. He had made the fire up and the dancing flames on the solar walls were playing with the shadows. He was becoming sleepy. Guy dared not fall asleep in case Gilbert accompanied George safely back to the solar.

When George returned, there was only Godfrey with him. Gilbert needed to talk with Rolf and Gunter about their findings in the forest, and it was important that they relayed what they had discovered. This was a good thing because Guy had almost fallen asleep; so, Godfrey helped George to get ready for his bed, and he urged Guy to put the bar across the door before he made ready for bed. He also warned to be abroad at the first light to avoid Gilbert finding him indisposed.

'Aye, my lord, I will do so,' he replied. Once Godfrey had left, Guy put the bar on the door and undressed and washed behind the screen ready for bed. Guy climbed onto his pallet. He would not let his grandfather down. Gilbert would think when he had gone that he had run away.

Chapter 5

Guy and George had broken their fast before Gilbert made his way to the thegn's solar to greet them.

'Good morning, how are you feeling this morning, George?' Gilbert asked.

'If you could excuse me, sir, I'm still a little weary. I'm sure Godfrey could fill in for me if there are matters to discuss. I will have Guy here to see to my needs.'

'Of course, George. I would not wish to cause you any more distress than necessary, and I'm certain after a rest you will be refreshed enough to take your supper with me.'

'Yes, I'm sure you are right, sir. There is no fun in old age.'

'Aye, you're quite right, George. So, it's you, me, and Gunter, Godfrey. If you could join me in the main hall when you have spoken with Guy to make sure he takes care and does not leave George unless he sends him on an errand. Wally was grumbling that Enid and Guy were dallying together last evening, making her late back to the kitchens.'

Gilbert left the solar smiling and shaking his head. Guy might be graceful and pretty, but he appeared close to Enid. He wasn't sure that Guy would be suitable for Enid. She would need someone brawny as she herself was only slight. He would need to keep his eyes on the situation; ultimately, it would be he that would have to give his blessing if at some point they wanted to marry.

Gilbert, Gunter and Godfrey took a small entourage of soldiers. There had been no sightings of renegades in the forest, but Gilbert wanted to be sure. He had left Rolf to supervise the erection of extra outdoor shelters.

The small party of soldiers and the knights searched every nook, cave, and cranny; no one was found. If there had been anyone lurking in the woods, they must have realised that William now had men residing at the manor house and would be alerted to anyone other than themselves hunting and hiding amongst the woods and caves. So, any renegades would have found that it would be safer to go further abroad in the woods than near to the manor house.

This gave Godfrey the news that they needed. They would soon be able sneak Guy out of the castle and get the child to safety. There would be too many Normans abroad on Saturday, the day of the feasting. He would advise George to wait another week. That way everyone would be working one way or another. He would report his findings on his return. Once they had a plan, they would make sure that Guy was fully conversant with what he would have to do. All Guy would have to do would be to follow instructions and to stay out of sight until Godfrey joined him.

As soon as possible, Godfrey imparted the news to George, saying that the Normans had declared the woods safe so they could now put their plan for Guy into action. Once advised of the plan, Guy was understandably upset.

'But, master, I wouldn't wish to leave you. I've managed so far without detection.'

'Guy, we can only keep your identity a secret for a short time. Sooner or later someone will notice or even one of our own could have a loose tongue. We need you to be removed out of harm's way as soon as possible.'

'But, master, I will miss you so.'

'Enough. You will obey me,' George held his hand up. It grieved him so to be harsh with his only grandchild. He too did not wish Guy to leave him, but he feared more what could happen if anyone found out his identity. He felt that he could feel the life draining out of him.

Godfrey intervened. 'Your master won't be here forever. Neither will I. We won't be able to protect you forever, and we will rest peacefully if we know you are protected.'

'I know, sir, but it will be so hard not to see you both again,' and the lavender blue eyes began to fill with tears.

'Wipe your eyes, Guy. I need to be strong myself. I too can't stand losing you. I promised your father to protect you and that I will do with Godfrey's help. Please do as you're told.'

'I'm sorry, master, I will.' Guy turned to fill a goblet of wine for George and Godfrey and tried to control himself by forcing a smile. By the time he turned around from his task, he looked much brighter, offering both George and Godfrey the freshly filled goblets of wine.

Soon Saturday was upon them and the feast was being prepared. Saxons would have to kneel at Gilbert's feet and swear fealty to him. He was sad that George Rowlands would be the first. If he could spare the elderly man, he would, but it was important that the serfs and churls saw him and Godfrey do so. He knew that to see their old master kneel would sweeten their thoughts. The ale and food would help it along. Anyone who did not wish to could leave his protection and make his way to a new area, but it would be hard on anyone doing so. Gilbert preferred his free men to stay at the village. If they were now free, it was because they could be trusted and worked well. These were the type of villagers any overlord would crave for.

George moved to the head of the queue, and Gunter quickly moved forward, a stool in his hands with a large cushion on.

'It will make it easier for you, sir,' he said with a smile. He too felt for George. Gunter helped him to kneel on one side, and Guy insisted he helped his master the other side. Once he had sworn fealty, he pulled Guy forward to kneel, and as he did so, he looked down on the ground.

Gilbert instructed, 'Look at me, boy,' and as Guy looked up at him, Gilbert not for the first time thought, I could drown in those eyes. So much so, he hardly heard his own words until he realised that Guy's voice was as sweet as any girl's. This mystified him all the more. Gilbert realised that they had been waging war for quite some time, and there had only been men for company, but surely, he must be able to control his thoughts. *I'd swear my brains have gone abegging where the lad is concerned.*

He soon pushed the thought out of his mind when one by one the whole of the village, including Godfrey, uttered the words of loyalty. By the side of Gilbert there was another chair padded with cushions. George had been helped to sit down on it and the stool placed for him to rest his feet upon.

The merrymaking went on until early in the morning. George had been forced to retire early as it became obvious that the elderly thegn was falling asleep.

Godfrey helped him up and George said, 'Goodnight, my lord, enjoy the rest of the merrymaking. We will meet again in the morning. I'm sure you will sleep well once you retire. It is a night for merrymaking.'

'Goodnight, George, sleep well. You too, Guy. And by the way, the seamstress says she already has your measurements and Wulf's as well, so you will soon have some new threads to wear. I'll wager they will be an improvement on what you are wearing, lad.' Nodding his head, he dismissed the small party as they made their way to the solar.

'That went better than I thought. Everyone appears to be happy including Percival. He no way expected to be given the job of castle reeve. He was very happy.'

Godfrey soon attended to George, and Guy once more was instructed to put the bar across the door and to make sure he was up and dressed in the morning as not to draw attention to himself. Guy took his bowl of water behind the screen to have a wash before retiring.

'Goodnight, master, sleep well.'

'You too, Guy. It won't be long now, and you will be safe.' Guy put another couple of logs on the fire. He had already given George a potion to help him sleep.

Going to the bed, he kissed the leathery cheek whispering, 'Goodnight, master.' Snuffing out all but one sconce, he made his way to his pallet. He had left one burning in case George needed a drink in the night. The light would make it easier for him to find the drink, or whatever George would need. Giving a small smile, he thought, *I think I am making a good serf. I must have taken heed of what Enid did when I was a small child.*

Lying on the bed, he was awake until the early morning, getting up when day was only just breaking and a thin light coming through the slats in the castle wall. He then dressed and washed his face. Once this was done, he took the bar off the door and ventured into the passage. There were still a number of sconces burning. Holding up a bundle of rushes, he lit it and returned to the fire placing rushes off the floor into the grate and placing them onto the lit bundle.

He soon had a good fire going for George after adding logs. Gathering the rest, he placed them in the fire opening and put more logs on the now blazing rushes. Taking a broom, he placed it in readiness to sweep the floor. Before he swept the floor, he needed to put a can on the hook to warm some water for George to wash. He himself could use cold water. George needed something to keep him warm. His bones were old and frail, and sometimes he was even cold when he had thick woollen threads on, as well as extra woollen undergarments.

Guy soon had the floor swept and some fresh rushes on the floor. Finding a bunch of sweet-smelling herbs that had been dried, he then dropped them into the rushes. The chamber soon felt warm and the perfume of the herbs assailed his nostrils. George was still sleeping, so he sat on a stool looking into the flames. How was he going to manage without his much-loved grandfather?

Finding a clean tunic for George, he placed it where it would warm for him. Most of all, would Grandfather manage without him? He quickly found the answer. Gilbert was kind, and he was sure the old man would be well looked after. Why did Godfrey and George worry that he wouldn't have looked after him as well, he couldn't understand. Gilbert appeared to be kind to all of them.

Sitting there, he had asked Enid to bring gruel for George's breakfast. He couldn't always digest meat; the gruel would be better for him and perhaps build him up a little. Guy was aware how his grandfather had lost weight.

Deep in thought, Guy was suddenly aware that there was a scratching at the door. It must be Enid, he thought. Quickly going to the door, he was smiling as he opened it. He was staring into the grey eyes of Gilbert Bayeux and try as he might, he couldn't drag his gaze away; his heart seemed like a trapped bird wanting to escape his chest. It was Gilbert who looked away first, once more wondering why this young man occupied his mind so much. It was setting his mind thinking it was something he needed to look into, but why?

Staring over Guy's head, he asked, 'Is your master still resting, Guy?' and at the same time walking over to the bed gazing down at the old man.

'I will wake him when Enid comes with his food, my lord.' Looking around the chamber, he noticed the roaring fire and the fresh rushes on the floor.

'I'll wager you have been awake for quite a while, Guy. I've heard you moving about. My fire is not yet lit, and it smells good in here. I can understand now why you grow sweet-smelling herbs to place on the floor.' Gilbert stopped himself saying anymore. He was about to tell Guy that when George passed, he would take him as one of his pages along with Wulf. He decided it would keep. He could wager that when George's passing came about that Guy would take it harder than even Godfrey who was George's old friend.

Once more, Gilbert thought these Saxon serfs were loyal to their masters. He had known many in Normandy that would sell their master's life for a piece of gold. The Saxons not so; they would lay down their life if their master was good, and George appeared to be a very good master. He had witnessed clear evidence amongst the villagers.

'I'll leave you in peace. Tell George I'll see him before I ride around the village to inspect the strips of land. If he feels like keeping me company, he will be most welcome.'

'Yes, my lord,' Guy answered keeping his head down.

'I will come back to wish him good morning and will have a gentle mare for him to ride if he so wishes.' With a nod of the head, he was gone, passing Enid as he went.

Dammit, why do I want to stay around the lad? he thought. He wasn't that short of a maid. Although if William decided to visit, he would look to see if any maid in Matilda's ladies in waiting took his fancy. It had been a while, but he had been busy fighting. Yes, he had more time to think; that was it. Rubbing his chin, he thought, yes it was time he married, then he would have a wife in his bed. It would control his wandering thoughts and satisfy his bodily needs.

He had noticed over the last two or three weeks that Gunter seemed to be watching Enid, and yes, she was a comely maid. Gunter would make her a much more suitable man than Guy. Gunter must also be feeling the same as himself after the long war. He didn't wish that Guy be hurt though for he had a liking for the puny lad.

Enid placed the tray holding the trencher with bread and a bowl of gruel, a flagon of ale and two fresh goblets. George was just stirring.

'It's nice and warm in here, Guy.'

'Yes, I've been awake for a while. Master, your breakfast is here. Let us get some water for you to wash your hands, then you can break your fast and be dressed before his Lord Gilbert returns.'

'He's been here already, Guy?' he asked giving Guy a sharp look.

'Yes, master, he will be back in an hour to see if you would like to ride to through the village with him.'

'Then I must make haste and dress ready if he is to return.'

'He will give you plenty of time, master. Here, wash your hands and eat your food. I have your tunic warming.'

Guy then bundled up the washing for Enid to take with her to the wash house. Quickly taking some bread and a small amount of ale, Guy wasn't very hungry. He was still slightly upset by the thought of leaving; however, he had always obeyed his grandfather, and he must still do so.

Besides, he wasn't sure that at some point he might let his grandfather down every time he was in Gilbert's company. He felt drawn to him, and he did like him. He was tall, strong and he would wager as brave as any knight in the stories they told. However, he did not want to let his grandfather down and put him in danger. He must be careful while he was at the manor. The Lord Gilbert appeared to be most observant. Having a little time to think, Guy tried to think why he liked Gilbert other than him being kind and considerate. Well, he thought, every time he entered their solar, he seemed to fill it with his height and breadth. He also could see the rippling muscles underneath his tunic and if outside or in the firelight, his hair shone as white gold. If the sun was on it, it turned red with the rays, and his grey eyes appeared to change from silver to stormy grey.

Guy had to pull himself from his daydreaming as his grandfather said, 'I've finished, Guy. I would like to wash now.'

'Yes, master,' he replied as he rose to prepare fresh warm water for George.

Very soon Guy had George dressed and washed and sitting in the chair by the fire. Guy found his warm cloak and a hat. He would be okay wrapped up. Spring was in the air, but it was slightly warmer and the thegn would perhaps benefit by the fresh air.

True to his word, Gilbert came back, 'Good morning, George. I take it Guy told you I intend to ride around the village and inspect the land. It would please me if you feel well enough to accompany me.'

'I would like that, Gilbert.'

'Good, I've already had a horse saddled and ready for you. Shall we go?' Guy jumped up and helped George with his cloak and gave him a hat.

Walking at the side of George, Guy felt Gilbert's eyes on him. Not daring to look, he walked at the side of

George without speaking. Gilbert could only puzzle over why Guy was bothering him. Every time he looked into the lavender blue eyes, he felt this urge to have speech with him. He hadn't felt that way about any of the other serfs in the village. Holy Mother, he thought, what was getting into him.

Walking across the courtyard, they had hardly reached the stable when a horse broke free from his groom to trot sedately to Guy, nuzzling into Guy's neck. Guy kissed the horse and appeared to be overjoyed to see him, as the horse was to see him. Guy appeared to have forgotten the two men as he stroked the mare's neck and whispered sweet words into the mare's coat.

Gilbert stood and looked amazed. The horse appeared to be used to Guy. Before Gilbert could comment, George said, 'Have you been feeding the mares apples again, Guy? I've told you before if they are green and sour they will give them colic. Leave the feeding to the grooms boy,' he said in a stern voice.

'Take the mare back into the stable, and I'll help your master to mount,' came Gilbert's instruction feeling a little angry with himself. For some reason he couldn't turn his anger on the boy.

A quiet destrier had been ready for George, while the one that had been saddled and ready for Gilbert was a large black destrier that was both feisty and obviously of a stronger character. Steam blew down its nostrils as it pawed the ground ready for his master to mount. This horse was only used to his master. Lord Gilbert's own mount would take a strong hand to control him and watching Gilbert, George realised that the horse would only be controlled by his master. The knight obviously rode well and needed a strong fast horse. And would be an accomplished horseman. A thought came into George's head that even as a young man he wouldn't have liked to do battle with this knight. He would be a hard adversary to contend with.

Guy came out to see Gilbert and George ride away. Guy was worried and hoped that Gilbert would look after Grandfather as he would, and straight away the notion came to him that Grandfather would be safe in Gilbert's hands. He only ever appeared to kind with his grandfather. Still, it wouldn't stop him worrying about him until he was back in the solar resting.

Making his way back from the stables to the manor, he stopped off at the kitchens for a word with Enid asking her to pick some herbs and lettuce to make a sleeping potion for George to help him sleep. He didn't dare do it himself in case he was found making it. There seemed to be Normans everywhere. They were in an adjoining field honing their sword skills and firing arrows at targets to ensure if they had to fight again, they would be ready to move and be able to protect themselves from the enemy. *This is understandable, but why did they have to take Grandfather's manor?* he wrestled in his mind. *Why couldn't they leave us in peace? Grandfather would be no threat to them.* Once more the answer flew to his mind. It was because they would be at the mercy of any marauding renegade soldiers. All their fit men had died at Harold's side. The men and boys they had left were not skilled in fighting, only farming and general labour. At least the castle had strong fighting men to protect them now.

Guy made his way back to the solar never feeling at ease if he wasn't inside. He really should have been making the most of the time he had left with his grandfather. All he had wanted to do was to ride abroad on his mare, Star. If pushed when riding, she was as fast as any mare in the stable despite being gentle and easy for him to handle.

How Guy wished for the carefree days that Enid, Wulf and his brother who had perished at the side of his father, would play games in the woods. Hoodwink Blind had been one of Guy's favourite games. His brother was slightly older than him and had been jubilant once he had persuaded a reluctant father to allow him to fight at his side, only to perish at his side. If he had not gone, it might have been harder for him as he would have been the heir to Alder-Sea. As the younger child, Guy was angry. His brother would have been worse.

Peering into the chest, he readied a small bundle of clothing to carry into the woods once his grandfather bid him to. He hid it at the bottom of the chest in readiness. Enid was to supply some extra food at the suppertime. This was to be carried in a small linen bag. This would hang quite well on the pommel of the mount, enough for him and Godfrey. Guy had no idea what his life would be like when he left here, thinking he would put up with anything as long as he was still with George.

He would miss his grandfather and possibly never see him again. His mind slipped onto his new Lord Gilbert. Aye, he would miss him too, as well as Rolf and Gunter who always had a kind word for him and Grandfather. Aye, he would miss the Norman knights. They seemed to wrap their strength around them making him feel safe. He couldn't help but think that they had been demonised without a hearing. He then felt guilty. Had not his father Richard Rowlands and brother Alfred died at the hands of the Norman knights? Yet he still couldn't hate them.

Guy found himself thinking of Gilbert. He tried to stop himself but couldn't. He was sure his grandfather would be angry if he knew that he liked Gilbert, so he needed to keep his own counsel and bury it deep and not have such thoughts. At sixteen, the serfs and churls were considered grown men and maidens where he, Guy, was treated as a child. He couldn't help but think he was being treated unfairly. If he could be himself, he would probably turn more than one head. Aye, he remembered one visitor to the castle telling him he was beautiful and that was indeed a compliment.

He stocked the fire up ready for Grandfather's return. Guy was sure he would be chilled since the wind was quite cold and gusty outside. He placed a jug of spiced wine in readiness for his return. The warm wine would help as well. Enid was soon back with the mixed herbs to help Grandfather to sleep after he had supped tonight.

Guy could relax now he had readied himself for his master's return, thinking he was also ready to be the obedient grandchild. Avoiding distressing his grandfather, if he realised he was upset, this in turn would upset Grandfather and that wasn't what Guy wanted. He hoped his grandfather would feel peace once he had him in the priory safe. He knew it would be a long time before he would feel peace, and he longed to stay with his grandfather. He had no wish to leave him and would spend his time wanting to be back living with him. Guy had no wish to live at the priory.

Enid entered the solar and advised, 'Lord Gilbert is on his way. He is helping my lord back as we speak.'

Getting up, Guy said, 'Thanks for letting me know. I had better check that I have enough goblets to offer my Lord Gilbert a warming drink as well. He's sure to have felt the chill today. The wind was quite cold and blustery.' Busying himself in finding the goblets and ensuring they were clean and in readiness for the returning party, he sat down once more, ready to spring up as they approached the door. He sat listening intently for the footfall along the long passage to the solar, jumping to his feet as he heard the soft tread. The door was thick and kept out the main noise.

Soon after Enid had left the chamber, the door opened once more and the small party of Gilbert, Godfrey and George walked in. George was being supported by the two knights. Gilbert loosened his cloak before helping him to lower himself into his chair.

Guy quietly picked up the warmed wine flagon and preceded to pass his Lord Gilbert and Godfrey a goblet. Picking the third up, Guy held the warmed wine to the elderly man's lips. George sipped a little and allowed Guy to support the goblet as his hands were weak. Guy wiped away any spillage that ran down his chin with the cloth he had used to pick up the hot flagon off the hearth. Guy realised that his grandfather had partaken his fill as he leaned back and his eyes closed as he caught his breath.

What a strange lad, Gilbert thought as he noticed the huge violet blue eyes appear to fill with tears. Perhaps the lad had waited on George for a while. He did seem unusually attached to his master, but tears! It was obvious that they needed to make George as comfortable as possible, and afterwards, he needed to make sure the young boy toughened up a little, or he wouldn't have a good life. He would be the butt of people's jokes. And he, Gilbert Bayeux, had promised to protect and look after all at Castle Alder-sea, strong and weak alike. Something inside him told him that Guy would be his special project and strangely, that he wanted to keep him close, once more shaking his head at such thoughts.

George was too frail to take supper in the main hall that night. Godfrey passed George's apology on to Gilbert when he went to join him for supper, leaving shortly after he had finished his supper, saying that he would spend a little time with George before he slept. Sometimes company without speech made for a good sleep if one did not feel well. He made Gilbert aware without actually saying that George's life was ebbing away.

'Goodnight, my lord. I will see you tomorrow and complete any tasks that I need to attend to.' Gilbert wished him a goodnight and turned his attention to two soldiers arguing with a Saxon elder. He needed to make sure it was only a small disagreement and would not erupt into anything more ominous. Gilbert patiently sat and watched the soldiers until they were once more jesting with the Saxon, and he was soon satisfied all was well.

Making his way back to George, Godfrey knew that he would be trusted at sometime this week with guiding the child to a priory, carrying a dowery as well. He would have to be very alert and travel early hoping that he would return quickly. There was a priory quite near, but fifty miles away. The child was a good rider and would keep up with him on Star, his mare, as the mare would acquit itself well.

Striding down the corridor to George's solar, he checked that no one was abroad in the long passageway to listen in on any speech with George. Once he was certain that everyone was engaged elsewhere, he entered his thegn's room. Dragging a chair close to the bed, he watched the shallow breathing of George. As George's eyes flickered open, he waved Godfrey closer to him.

'The time has arrived. We need to put our plan into action before daybreak tomorrow. The child must walk the passage and hide in the shelter of the covering trees and lynch that hang. Take the dowery and hide it in your clothing. You can ride on one horse. Someone might think it is suspicious if you take a spare horse out with you.'

'Yes, my lord.'

'The child is light and will not try the horse's strength too much.'

'It will be done, my old friend, and I will keep Guy safe. I will be back before anyone misses me.'

'If either of you are discovered in the forest, you must tell them you are looking for early fruit for breaking my fast.'

'Yes, my lord, I will guard him with my very life.'

'I know you will, my good friend. May the Holy Mother watch over you both and keep you safe from harm.'

Guy's eyes were full of sorrow. He knew the time was here, and he must obey his beloved grandfather, the only person left of his family. How was he going to bear such sorrow of leaving him?

Godfrey quickly put his fingers to his lips as he heard his Lord Gilbert approaching the solar. He was also sure that Gilbert would come in to see all was well with George. He quickly passed Guy a length of cloth and motioned him to dry his eyes. It would not be seemly for a young lad to show to much emotion. Guy pulled himself together in the nick of time, as Gilbert was soon upon them. He had taken the cloth and quickly wiped his eyes.

Guy stood and attended to the fire as Gilbert entered with Rolf, Gunter having been dispatched to inspect that the guards were sufficient for the castle safety.

'How is he, Godfrey?'

'Not well, Gilbert. He is very frail. He has good days and bad days, and this is one of the bad days.'

'Perhaps it would be prudent for him to stay abed tomorrow. He will have Guy in attendance, and you can stay close tomorrow, Godfrey.'

'Thank you, Gilbert. I would like that. It is kind of you. Perhaps once he is rested, he will recover a little.'

'If he becomes worse or the lad needs help with him, I will have Wulf ready at your request to help.' Gilbert wanted to give Guy a kind word; however, it might have appeared strange for him to be taking such an interest in the young lad, so bidding Godfrey to keep him informed of George's progress, he left to go about his business as there was still quite a lot to be attended to.

Without George at his side, he would need all his powers of concentration to deal with it. There would still be the odd one out that would look upon him with suspicion. This he needed to contain and with the almighty's help, he would endeavour to turn them to his way of thinking.

Once Gilbert had left, Godfrey quietly went over the plan with Guy for him to leave via the secret passageway under the large tapestry hanging on the wall. He himself would come early when the light was just filtering in and see Guy through the passage door. He would make sure he had his bundle of clothes and a light. He would alert Enid to provide bread and drink and George's breakfast early before the castle was abroad. He would be there to see Guy in the passageway and to close the door after him. And he would stay in the solar until he was sure that Gilbert would not visit George to check on him in the morning. As soon as he thought the coast was clear, he would make his way to the dell and ride swiftly to the priory, therefore ensuring that Guy was safe at last.

'One more thing, Guy. If we are discovered, we must give the excuse we were looking for early fruits for the master and had carried our breakfast with us.'

Finding the gold for the dowery, Godfrey secreted it in his clothing in small pockets so there was no large bulge of a money bag. They would stop near to the priory for

Guy to change his clothes and at the same time he could put the gold in one container for the prioress.

'Put the bar across, Guy, and I will be back. Don't go to bed. I will be but a short time and if no one is about, I'll bring the food with me to save Enid being here in the morning.' Guy watched as Godfrey quietly left the solar, placing the bar back in place. Sitting down by the fire, he placed another log on the fire to keep the solar warm for George. Guy then sat down to keep his vigil over his grandfather. Inside, his heart was breaking as he watched the elderly man sleeping.

True to word, Godfrey was soon back carrying a full bag of food and drink for tomorrow. He had enough for breakfast and plenty for the journey on the morrow.

'I'll sleep in here tonight, Guy. I want nought to go wrong. You have everything clear in your head now, Guy?' Godfrey asked.

'Aye, I have, although I will miss you both so much.'

'No more than we will you. Your grandfather's heart will be the happier to know you are safe. Now get some sleep.'

'I will, but you take the pallet. I will make myself comfortable at Grandfather's side. I have washed while you were collecting the food.'

'Goodnight, child,' Godfrey whispered even though the solar walls were around four feet thick and once in the next solar naught could be heard. Snuffing out the sconces except one, they put more logs on the fire. Their sleep would be short, and they needed to keep it burning if they could. Guy carefully lay at the side of his grandfather while Godfrey took off his belt and sword and unlaced his boots and lay upon the pallet. Morning would be short in arriving, and they needed to be alert.

It mattered not to Godfrey that he could be punished for keeping the secret of Guy's birth from Gilbert. He, like George, had lived for many years. They were in the winter of their life. Neither had many years stretching in front of them, and Godfrey would be happy if he could serve his old friend by completing this one task for him. It would mean that he would go to his maker a happy man.

George had made Godfrey feel like family. They had consoled each other when they lost their family for he too had sons that had perished fighting at Harold's side. He would miss his old friend. He realised that his time was short. It perhaps wouldn't be long before he joined George, for he was now tired as well. Godfrey himself had seen enough of war and its outcome of changing people's lives.

Lying awake, Godfrey was aware that it would be a long night. Try as he might, he couldn't catch his sleep, and he was aware he needed to be alert tomorrow to carry out George's wishes successfully.

Chapter 6

Morning light was soon creeping into the solar and neither Godfrey nor Guy had managed to have much sleep. Their minds had been overthinking through the night. Guy was finding it nigh impossible to accept losing his grandfather who had taken care of him since his father had set out to fight at the side of Harold. Now why could they not ask Gilbert to allow him to continue to be his grandfather's ward? Surely, he would be as kind to him as Guy, or as George's grandson. What difference would it make? Guy was sad that he couldn't be accepted by Gilbert. There was something about him that both frightened and excited him, but now he would never know what.

Dressing warmly because he knew that he must walk the passageway soon, he put some more wood upon the fire for his grandfather. At least he would be warm in his chamber when he left. Once Godfrey returned, he was sure they would be safe. Guy liked to think he knew Lord Gilbert even though he had only known him a short while.

Going into the chest, he found his bundle of clothes to take with him. He looked at the bread that was covered for them to break their fast, and he knew he could not eat a morsel. It would stick in his throat. Picking up a goblet, he would just have a drink, that would be enough. He would be taking the food that had been tied together along the passage with him. If he was hungry later, he would have a bite of that.

Godfrey stirred. Looking at the slits in the wall, he realised what he must do.

Jumping off the pallet, he said, 'You should have woken me, Guy.'

'I wasn't sure, sir. I have gathered the bundle I must take along with our food parcel. I have had a drink, but it is too early for me to eat.'

'Nevertheless, you must take a little bread and cheese with you, as you will have a wait before I can join you.'

'I will stay in the shelter of the trees covering the entrance of the passage until I hear your horse approaching me.'

'Guy, make sure you stay well out of sight. There could be other people that inhabit the woods, not just the wolves.'

'Aye, I will, Godfrey, and I won't completely close the tunnel entrance until I hear you come, sir.'

'Good lad, we need to make sure that we carry out your grandfather's bidding to the letter, so his mind will then be at peace.'

'Well, the sooner I go the better, and you can join me when it is safe.' Walking over to George, Guy stood looking at his grandfather, memorising every wrinkle and furrow of his beloved face. Life would never be the same for Guy.

Bending down, he gently kissed George and said, 'I will always love you, Grandfather, and I swear I'll never forget you.'

'Come Guy, you need to go before anyone else is abroad,' Godfrey said. Lifting the tapestry, he opened the secret door in the wall. It made a slight grinding noise, and he hoped that it would not be heard in the other solar.

Lighting a bundle of rushes and tucking an extra unlit one through the knot of his bundle, Guy said, 'Thank you, Godfrey, and I will stay safe until you come to find me.' By now, Guy could not help the tears falling from his lavender blue eyes.

'Don't cry, child, we will soon have you safe. Think how happy it will make your grandfather. Now be off with you until I can join you. May God watch over you.' With that, Godfrey gave Guy a gentle push and closed the door behind him. Pulling the huge tapestry back in place, he walked over to George, who he sensed more than heard was awake until the child left.

Godfrey set about silently helping his old friend wash, both too full to discuss Guy leaving. They both loved Guy, and Godfrey had been like a great uncle watching over the child and helping to protect him. He would sorely miss him too.

Once George was dressed, he served him with a little ale and a portion of food. As Godfrey suspected, George ate very little. He took some fresh water to wash himself and put on his clothes. He then took the time to break a little bread himself. He also had little appetite, realising that he would soon lose the greatest and best friend he had. Who wouldn't be upset and sad at that? For it would be like losing part of his family, and they had all gone before him.

Going to the door, Godfrey took the bar away from the door, as his Lord Gilbert might find it strange that Guy had gone out and the door was still barred. All too soon, Gilbert's visit to see how George fared was there.

'Good morning, my lord, how do you fare today? Better, I hope.'

'A little, Gilbert. I will, however, rest until this evening when I hope to be well enough to dine in the hall with you.'

'Good, George, I will look forward to your company and yours too, Godfrey,' looking around he asked, 'Has Guy gone on an errand?'

'He went to the kitchens to see if they had a few berries and to fetch some gruel for George's breakfast. It will sit better in George's stomach. Bread is a little heavy.'

'Good, I will be out most of the day riding the village so I will see both of you at supper,' Gilbert advised them.

'That means I won't be missed for the two or three hours it will take me to transport the child to the priory. That is fortunate, George. With God's help, we will be successful in our mission.'

'You will need to give Gilbert time to go about his business, then it will be safe for you to slip away. Most of the soldiers will then be busy building the extra outside shelters.'

'Aye, I will, George. Trust me, all will be well with God's help.'

Godfrey sat another hour with George, aware that Guy would be now at the end of the tunnel and waiting on him.

'Will you be alright now, George? I'll try and make my way to Guy.'

'I will be the better for knowing that you will be guiding Guy to where he will be safe out of harm's way. I somehow think my Lord Gilbert would not hurt the child, but I can't be sure. Besides, if he stays here, there might be others that would do so.'

'I will be on my way then, George.'

'God speed, Godfrey. I pray that He will watch over you.' Godfrey smiled and looked down the corridor to see if anyone was about.

As the door closed behind Godfrey, George breathed a sigh and rested his head back on the pillow. He had been near to tears himself as he heard Guy leave, not being able to say goodbye to his precious grandchild. Lying there, he did not dare to give in to tears in case he had a visit from

Gilbert or one of his knights. He had to lie quietly hoping that all would be well with them.

Guy hated walking down the tunnel, stifling the easy cries that came to his lips as a mouse or a rat scuttled in his path as he disturbed them. It was dark and dank, and in some places, water ran down the cold walls and the cobwebs of time caught at his head and clothes. He would be glad when he arrived at the outer door. Once it was opened, he could let in some fresh air to get rid of the stale air and breathe more freely.

Listening for any noises at the end of the tunnel, he waited a moment or two before attempting to open the outside door. It had been a long time since it had been opened, and it squeaked. Guy thought it was quite loud; however, there seemed to be no movement outside. So, pushing a little more, he made enough room for him to slip out in the shadow of the trees.

Taking a huge gulp of fresh air, he was glad to be out, leaving enough room for him to squeeze back in if necessary. Grateful to be outside the tunnel even if the trees were quite thick and overgrown, he placed the bundle of clothing and food at his feet and settled down to wait. Taking the sealed pigskin of wine, he poured a little into a wooden beaker, and took out the extra cloth of bread and cheese that Godfrey had insisted he take with him as he had not eaten any breakfast. Ripping a little bread and cheese and picking up the cup of wine, he forced himself to eat a little. Replacing what was left, he waited patiently for Godfrey to join him. As it was, it became a long wait.

Godfrey went to the main hall, and it was empty. It wasn't until he walked out that he was stopped by Gunter.

'Godfrey, just the person I need. I need your opinion on where to situate the extra privy or if we might need two. If you could spare the time to accompany me to the site behind the dovecotes, we could put our heads together and agree where to put it.'

'Of course, Gunter.' The two men walked past the herb garden and onto the land beyond the dovecote.

After much deliberation, Godfrey said, 'It makes sense to add another two at the back. One on the left and one to the right, further back at the very end. It's slightly farther to walk but won't be near enough to offend the ladies.'

'I knew you would come up with the right place to please all, thank you, Godfrey. I will instruct the soldiers at work to start straight away.'

'Well, now you have that sorted, I will be about the tasks that I need to attend to. I will see you at supper, Gunter.' Both men raised their hands in salute and went their separate ways.

Godfrey tried not to look as if he was in a hurry as he made his way to the stables. His horse was ready and waiting for him to mount. Making his way slowly out of the castle grounds and towards the forest, he looked right and left to ensure no one was watching. He slowly made way to his tryst with Guy.

Chapter 7

Guy sat patiently inside the bower of trees listening for any sign of Godfrey arriving. It seemed a long time waiting. He felt sick to his stomach as he thought about his grandfather, wishing that he would wake up and it would have all been a dream. Suddenly, he heard the sound of hoofs on the ground. He let the mount get nearer before he left the safety of his cover. Deciding to come out of his hiding place to see if it was Godfrey, he left his bundle of clothes and food inside the safety of the trees ready to slip back to get them if it was his old friend. Sneaking out carefully just in case it wasn't him, he did his best to make as little noise as possible. Too late. It was Lord Gilbert on his huge destrier riding towards him. Looking at his face, he was aware he had been seen, as the horse and rider pranced towards him.

Gilbert's face was like thunder. 'What are you doing here, boy, when your master needs you?'

'I'm looking for early fruits for my master's gruel. He does like wild fruits, and they are somewhat scarce at the moment,' Guy replied. Gilbert looked at the boy in front of him and knew that he shouldn't be having the thoughts that he had.

He felt furious with himself, almost snarling at the lad, 'Get back to the manor, boy, before I give you a good whipping. Do you not know better than to come this far out on your own or know what could befall you?' He was angry with himself for being upset that the lad might have been hurt, and if he hadn't come upon him, he might have met the wrong person, and he could have forfeited with his life. Gilbert's anger was great. This was unlike him. He would have just cuffed any other lad's ears. He just could not hurt this gentle and graceful lad, and it made him so angry that he couldn't.

'I didn't think, my lord,' Guy said, trying to hide his confusion. He wasn't sure if he felt frightened or elated as he stood in front of the imposing figure on the horse. He didn't feel scared at all, but he did feel something. What, he wasn't sure. Waiting in the bower for Godfrey to arrive was unnerving him. It was funny, he felt safe now. Yes, that was the feeling, he felt safe. This man that everyone had feared arriving at the manor was wrapping the whole of Castle Alder-sea and its lands in the safety of his arms. Guy looked up at him as he controlled the destrier to avoid trampling Guy under its hooves.

Gilbert had to control his wandering thoughts, 'I said back to the manor now, lad, before I do something I will regret.' Guy realised that he was being serious.

'Yes, my lord,' he whispered, turning and breaking into a run as Gilbert shouted, 'I will be right behind you, so no more diversions! Straight to the manor!' Guy made haste back to the manor well aware since he could hear the steady hooves and the snorting of the destrier that carried Gilbert behind him.

As Guy ran forward, he almost ran into Godfrey's horse. Looking at him, he realised that he had also spotted Gilbert, 'What are you doing, Guy?' he asked, 'We meant for you to look for fruit in the manor grounds. You have wandered too far out.'

'I'm sorry, sir. I couldn't find any, and I didn't realise that I had wandered so far.'

'Well, back to your master, boy, he was asking about you,' he said, looking at Gilbert riding towards him.

'Yes, my lord,' he quickly answered.

'Godfrey, you need to press upon Guy that he must stay by his master while he is ill. No good will come of him wandering the woods on his own.'

'Quite right, Gilbert, I will, along with George, make sure that he is aware that he needs to stay within the manor grounds.'

'By the holy saints, is he not aware of what dangers could befall a puny lad like him in these woods? We haven't come across any renegade bands but that doesn't say there are none. George will have to keep a firmer hand on him.'

'My Lord George and I will make sure he does not repeat today's escapades, Gilbert. I'll make it my task to ensure he stays within the confines of the manor grounds, and I'm sure it would just be an oversight on his part.'

'Let's have no more speech about it then, Godfrey. I trust your judgement,' Gilbert answered.

Why was he so upset to find Guy in the woods? Even now he could not understand his feelings. He wanted to protect this child. Was he a child? He understood that Guy had just passed his sixteenth year and would be expected to toil in the fields or other work at that age. Indeed, children of seven or eight were working the field. He had noted the slim, soft hands of the boy, and it intrigued him that a young lad had no signs of hard work being done by him. *Why?* he asked himself.

Shaking his head, he rode at the side of Godfrey in silence. He was ready for some refreshment; however, he decided to guide his horse to the land beyond the dovecotes to check how the work was coming along.

'You need to go to Guy and ensure that he is attending to George, and at the same time, you need to have speech with that lad about his duties.'

'Yes, Gilbert, I surely will.'

Gilbert rode away wondering why this lad hadn't toiled like other lads. He wasn't simple, it was obvious Guy understood what he was doing. A serf, especially a boy, would by now have learnt to work hard. Guy's duties appeared to be light, and he had noticed that he had joined in with speech when it wasn't his place to. Still, when George passed, he would see that Guy was trained properly and made into the man he should be, mayhap he had been coddled too much.

He would sorely miss George when he did. The short time he had known George, he liked him and felt sorry for the loss of his sons. He looked on him as a father figure because his father and mother were so far away. Godfrey was a kind loyal friend to George, and he too would take George's passing hard.

Godfrey and Guy strode into the solar, and George was astonished when he saw Guy was still on the castle grounds. Godfrey held his hand up without speaking as he glanced behind him into the corridor to ensure that they had not been followed.

Godfrey said, 'Tell us quietly what happened, Guy. I'm at loss myself as to why Gilbert found you.'

'I heard the horse coming, and I thought it must be you, so I came out of the bower and was nearly trampled under Lord Gilbert's destrier as he stamped and snorted as I appeared.'

'Did he see where you came from, lad?' George asked.

'No, master, I slipped out, and he didn't see me until I was in the clearing of the dell. I had no time to slip back without him seeing me.'

'So, he didn't see you by the tunnel?'

'No, master, I was careful.'

'But not careful enough. We should have been on our way by now,' Godfrey replied.

'Gilbert obviously was checking the perimeter of the castle. It happens to be most unfortunate that he rode at that time in the area you were to meet,' came George's analysis.

'We must learn by our mistakes, Guy. We will leave it a couple of days and try again. We must make sure that we are successful the next time. We cannot have Gilbert suspecting that something is afoot,' Godfrey quietly added.

'Aye, next time we will have to ensure our plan works, and to make sure that Gilbert doesn't catch us out again, you will need to stay in the safety of the tunnel or hidden in the bower of the trees.' George leant back in the chair that he was sitting, his strength already spent. His breath came in short gasps, 'A drink, Guy,' he whispered as he fought for breath.

Godfrey was quicker than Guy. He soon had a strong elixir that the cook brewed and he held the cup to George's lips. The old thegn had taken his last breath, and the drink just spilled from his lips. The fact that the plan hadn't worked had been too much for Guy's grandfather. And Guy didn't dare to let the tears that were burning at the back of his eyes fall. He just stood and held George's hand.

As he did so, he whispered, 'I love you, Grandfather.' There was no one other than Godfrey to hear the whispered cry of the wounded child. Godfrey felt for the child, but his sorrow went deep as well. He loved his old friend and the same as Guy, he was left without any family. He would attempt to get the child away for his old friend's sake. Then whatever happened to him didn't matter. He was willing to go to join his master. Placing his hand on the child's shoulder, he let a few minutes pass as he fought to control his grief.

'Guy, we must have speech now. I still need to carry out George's wishes, and we need to carry them out as soon as possible. I need to take you to the priory before who you are is discovered. The new lord is no fool. He appears to watch you.'

'Yes, my lord.'

'I think we are safe until after George is buried and a service held. He will look at placing you in some sort of job or position.'

'But what, Godfrey? I'm not skilled at outside work.'

'Although I think up to a point he is fair in judgement, he might not look kindly on being duped.'

'No, Godfrey, he is kind, but no one likes to be tricked,' Guy said, his blue eyes appearing huge in his face.

'My chamber is small; I will try and persuade the lord that we put you in my chamber, and I lay George out in here until he is buried.'

'Yes,' came Guy's short answer.

'If we can plan for you and me to slip in, I can then let you through the tunnel and shut the door after you.'

'Will we manage that, Godfrey?'

'Yes, I'm sure we will have the opportunity, and of course, you will have to be patient and perhaps stay at the tunnel opening longer until I can join you.'

'I will stay in the foliage, my lord.'

'Though you do realise you must not show yourself as you did before or all is lost.'

'Yes,' came the short answer. The boy squeezed his lavender blue eyes trying to will himself not to cry, but the tears could not be stopped.

Godfrey put his arms around Guy. 'You must control how you feel, child. We must not feed their thoughts if I am to obey your grandfather and protect both of us. We must be strong. So, for your sake as well as my own, you must make this the last of your grief, for it is a grief we are united in. I feel the loss of George as much as you, and we must not let it be the undoing of us.'

Going over to a bowl of cold water, Guy hastily washed the sign of tears away.

Refreshing the bowl with more water and clean cloth, he advised Godfrey, 'We must wash him for when he meets his maker. He was a proud man.' Guy busied himself getting the water ready with some sweet-smelling soap that they made from animal fat sweetened with the herbs that they grew in the small garden near the dovecotes. Carrying the bowel over to his grandfather, Guy made ready to wash him.

'Here, you give me that, and I'll wash him. You find some linen to wrap him in. Lay it out on the bed, and then I can place him onto it.'

Guy walked over and kissed his grandfather's cheek and obediently went over to one of the chests. Taking out a large piece of linen, he carefully tidied the bed and then lay the sheeting upon it. Godfrey gently undressed the emancipated body of his Lord George. Guy busied himself in finding his grandfather's best tunic and breeches. Passing them to Godfrey, he then looked for his neck chain with the emblem of his office. Grandfather had died quietly with just Godfrey and himself present. Guy was not going to let him be buried without the standard of his office being recognised; that was the least they could do. Godfrey carried his late master and good friend, placing him gently upon the clean expanse of linen and continued to redress him. Taking the tunic and the emblem of his nobility, he carefully dressed him, crossing his hands on his chest and placing coins on his closed eyes.

Guy and Godfrey had only just finished laying him out in his clothes of office and loosely wrapped the linen around him, when a scratching on the door was heard. Guy walked over and opened it. Gilbert Bayeux stood waiting to enter. Walking past Guy, he entered. The smile of greeting disappeared as he saw the freshly washed body dressed in his finery with his hands crossed on his chest.

Turning to Godfrey he asked, 'When?'

'Shortly after you returned with him, Gilbert.'

'Guy, this is why I told you that you should not have left your master,' he bit out angrily. Looking at the tears that suddenly appeared in the boy's eyes, he thought his words had struck home hard as the words he had spoken had been somewhat harsh.

'Gilbert, I have already chastised the boy. He was very fond of George. Please don't be too hard on him, my lord.'

'I'm sorry, but I too in the short time I have been here become very fond of George. He reminded me somewhat of my grandfather, and I looked forward to many weeks of time and speech with him. Now to become friends is not possible, and I had hoped that would be the case.

'Godfrey, I will have George taken to one of the chapels to lie in state for the next couple of days. You may occupy this solar with Guy until I've placed him in a suitable position. We can't put him to work outside. It wouldn't suit him, and he needs looking after. I entrust him to your care until we can place him,' he said in a more conciliatory tone.

Godfrey bowed. 'As you wish, my lord. Could I be excused at supper, my lord? I too feel the hurt from losing my old master and friend quite deeply. I would not like to spoil the ambience of tonight's supper, so if you don't mind, Gilbert, I will sup quietly with Guy and reflect.'

'Of course, Godfrey, you can sup in here. You might have lost one friend, but I would be pleased if you would consider me your friend as well for I feel we too will have many pleasant years together.'

'Thank you, Gilbert. I am fortunate indeed that you would consider me as a friend. You have been kindness itself to Guy and myself, and I assure you that we both appreciate your kindness in letting us stay in George's solar where we may feel close to him for a little longer.'

'It will give the lad time to get over his grief, as well as yourself. A brief interlude before we put him to rest,' Gilbert said gruffly.

'He was not just a good master but a great one, my lord. He will find his rest in eternity, and one day I'm sure we will meet again in the great unknown,' Godfrey replied.

'I will send serfs to take his body and lay it in state until we put him to rest. We will keep rushes lit and soldiers to guard his body. I'll also inform the kitchens to serve you supper in here, Godfrey,' and with a curt nod of his head, he was gone.

'Godfrey, could we wait until Grandfather is buried in the church yard before you take me to the priory? I would indeed like to see him put to rest,' the lad requested.

'No, Guy, I feel if we did, it might be your undoing. It is so obvious that you loved him, and if I have time to take you before the burial, I can feign not knowing where you have vanished to avoiding punishment myself.'

'Very well, my lord,' Guy answered his eyes downcast as he agreed.

'So, early tomorrow morning as before, we will let you into the tunnel. You will have a fresh bundle of clothes, and we will keep enough food from tonight's supper to carry with you. I will again wait until it is safe, and then we can ride as fast as we can to the priory.'

'Yes, my lord.'

'This way, we will have carried out your grandfather's wishes. You heard your Lord Gilbert. He intends to place you in some kind of work after they bury George,' he said sternly, hoping that Guy would understand why he was insisting on the time being now. Godfrey knew if he left it until after the burial that Gilbert would place Guy in some sort of meaningful employment and that he would soon find out their secret, and had he not knelt along with George and Guy and sworn allegiance at Gilbert's feet? No, he would sooner spirit Guy away than be looked on as a traitor. Godfrey was sure that his new master was a good man. He was torn by his pledge to George and although he liked and respected Gilbert, his loyalty was stronger to George.

The soldiers arrived and carried George to the chapel. Guy and Godfrey followed them to watch that George was laid in state in a caring manner, Guy being careful to whisper, 'Sleep well, master.' Godfrey stood and saluted him with his sword. One of the soldiers reported to Gilbert that there had been a suspicion of tears in Godfrey's eyes as he left the chapel and that the boy Guy was struggling with the Lord George's death. Strange for a boy so young.

Chapter 8

Soon suppertime arrived, and Enid delivered their supper.

'What have we, Enid?'

Looking at Godfrey, Enid said, 'I brought you a little extra, my lord. I thought you might like extra for breakfast.'

'That was good thinking, Enid. We will have the extra. Did you wrap it?'

'Yes, my lord, I have brought you a small muslin bag to carry it in.'

At this point Guy said, 'We really appreciate what you have done, Enid. I will miss you.'

'And I you, Guy. I wish there was some other way.'

'These are George's wishes, and we will carry them out, and I assure you we will all miss Guy; however, we must do this. Only then will his spirit rest.'

'It's alright, I understand it is Grandfather's wish, and I haven't disobeyed him before, and I promise I won't now.' Turning to look at the food basket, Guy successfully changed the subject by sorting the different dishes onto the small table. Enid sat and watched Guy silently. How she would miss her childhood friend.

'I best be getting back, or I'll feel the anger of cook. He will give me all the hard work if he feels that I have been chattering. May God go with you, Guy,' Enid said as tears sprung to her eyes. Quickly covering the distance between her and Guy, she hugged his slim form to her and ran from the solar. Screwing her fist in her eyes, she thought cook might be lenient with her. He would also be sorry that their old master had passed. The grief that they all felt was genuine as George also had a been a good master. And

Guy had always treated her as an equal and not one of the serf's children.

Meanwhile, Guy made up the bundle of clothes that he would need, and Godfrey silently placed a meat pastry and bread in the muslin bag along with a flagon of ale that would refresh them on their journey. Once things were prepared, they sat down to eat their supper and to take a drink of ale.

When they had finished their supper, Godfrey advised Guy that he needed to wash and get some rest. Tomorrow would be a stressful day, and they both needed to be alert before anyone was about.

'Yes, my lord,' Guy answered trying to stem the grief he was feeling.

Godfrey sat with his head in his hands by the fire as Guy silently washed behind the screen in the corner. Guy was trying not to think of having to walk that horrible passage again. The smell and the cobwebs had made him feel sick. Walk it he must. He hoped that it would give his grandfather peace in the hereafter. His thoughts were different. He couldn't help but wish that Godfrey and George had trusted Gilbert more. Neither of the good men were aware what type of man Gilbert would be.

There had been terrible attacks on other manor houses where their thegn had been killed in trying to defend their manors and families. Women had been killed and raped. What Godfrey had perceived on their first meeting was that Gilbert was a fair man, and he had been right. George, however, was bent on getting his grandchild away to safety. So, he had pledged to carry out George's wishes, as not even the Normans would attack a priory.

Early morning, Godfrey quietly said, 'Guy, it is time. You must get up and be on your way.' Guy got off the bed and dressed himself behind the screen, standing ready for Godfrey to open the tunnel entrance.

'Now don't come out of the bower over the door of the entrance until you hear my voice, understand?'

'Yes, Godfrey, I do.'

'Now, you might have to wait a short time, but I will be as quick as I can.' Guy just nodded his head in understanding and turned to enter the tunnel entrance.

He carefully made his way once more down the gloomy and dank tunnel, at the same time pulling the cobwebs away from his face as they stuck to his skin. He hated having to walk the distance to the door. Kicking out at a mouse in distaste that ran across his feet, he would soon get to the end, he thought, and he could breathe in that clean fresh air of the forest.

At last, he had reached the end of the tunnel. Picking up the bundle from yesterday, he reached in and took out the clothes. He could fit them in the bundle at the bottom. Mayhap they would be useful at the priory. The food he placed to one side. That would do for the small animals in the forest to scavenge when he had left.

Now the first part was accomplished, he was at the end pushing the door open and gulping the fresh air. He stayed just inside the tunnel for a short while listening to the noises in the forest. Once he felt safe, he ventured out and sat down not moving out of the safety of the bower. Reaching into the muslin bag, he forced himself to eat a little bread and meat and took a drink of ale.

Sitting on the soft moss beneath the screen of green foliage, he started his vigil waiting for Godfrey to appear. Whatever happened now, he could only hold onto his grandfather within his memory along with his father's. Guy couldn't remember his mother since she had died when he was born. Now he only had memories of his kind and gentle grandfather. He would also never forget his childhood friends. Enid the most; they had been close always deciding together what they would do in play for the day. Sadly, those days were no more. He had to forget and become the grownup that he should be. Soon, he would reside with strangers.

He suddenly thought he would have liked to stay safely with Gilbert. He was sure he would have cared for him although Grandfather had preferred to be sure, Guy thought, in case Gilbert would not have liked him. Now the dye was cast, and there was no turning back. He was sure Gilbert was kind, and his harsh words he had spoken to him had not been of character. He had felt for Grandfather. But then again, his grandfather had also been easy to love, and he also had been kind and gentle. He occasionally had also been harsh, but only when pushed.

Guy smiled quietly to himself. They all had pushed Grandfather to his limits, even Enid. They were always being warned not to wander away from the village. Somehow, they could not quite keep that fact in their minds and would wander deep into the woods to play their childish dreams out as fair maidens that needed to be rescued by handsome knights who would carry them away on their huge chargers.

He sat there with tears running silently down his face as he suddenly realised he would never see his beloved grandfather again. How he wished that Grandfather was still here to scold him. He would never disobey him again if he could just have him back.

'I love you, Grandfather. Why did you have to leave me?' he whispered in his grief.

As he sat quietly, he managed to control his grief once more, warning himself that he must not be heard.

It seemed an awful long time before he heard Godfrey's quiet voice saying, 'Guy, I am here.'

Guy looked through the dense boughs of the bushes, and whispered, 'I will shut the tunnel door, my lord.' Turning back, he was soon closing the door and picking up his bundle of clothes, making his way out of the trees. He passed Godfrey the clothes and the food that he soon had hanging on the pommel of his saddle. Leaning down towards Guy, he pulled him up onto the back of his destrier.

'Are you comfortable, Guy?' he asked.

'Yes, my Lord Godfrey, I'm quite comfortable,' came the answer.

'Then we must make haste if I am to be back before I'm discovered missing,' and with a touch of his heels in the flanks of the destrier, they were away.

They hadn't got far before they heard the thud of hooves behind them. They were being pursued by three large destriers ridden by renegade soldiers.

'Hold on, child,' Godfrey instructed Guy as he urged his horse to go faster. It was too late to weave or avoid the missile as he heard the whistle of an arrow hit his shoulder, knocking him from his horse, and rendering him senseless and falling to the floor. Guy had fallen with him, his head striking a rock.

The renegade soldiers slewed their horses and slid from their backs. Just as they were about to attack the elderly knight and do him more damage, more arrows hit their targets thudding into the attacking renegade soldiers, but not before one had attempted to stab Godfrey as he lay powerless at his feet. Fortunately for Godfrey, the wound was a flesh wound and had not punctured any vital organs. But the loss of blood for the old knight was too much, and he passed out. The knights and the little band of soldiers brought their horses to a halt and slid to the ground.

It had been lucky for them that the day before it had been reported that they had found signs of renegade soldiers within the forest so Gilbert, Rolf and a small band of soldiers had set out to root them out of the forest. Gilbert's and Rolf's arrows had been more deadly; two of the attackers lay dead beside Guy and Godfrey.

Gilbert was the first down and kneeling at the side of Guy and feeling for a pulse, 'Thanks to the Holy Mother the boy is just senseless. He has suffered a huge blow to the head. Rolf, how fares my Lord Godfrey?'

'He has lost a lot of blood, Gilbert. He has been hit by an arrow. It's bad but it appears to have missed his heart, and he also has a knife wound.'

'We need to get them back to the manor quickly and carefully. You there, take the wounded attacker and bind him on his horse. He needs to be put into the guardhouse until we can try him for his crimes.'

'Yes, my lord,' came the soldier's answer.

'Rolf, you have the Lord Godfrey placed upon your horse in front of you. Be gentle with him. He too is of great age. I will want to know what they were doing deep in the forest this hour of the day. I will take the boy, and it will keep until they regain their senses along with some of their strength. We need to know whether the boy wandered off on his own and Godfrey sought to cover up for him. He needs to understand he cannot bend the rules,' he said thoughtfully.

'It indeed does seem strange, Gilbert. Do you think there is something afoot?'

'I hope not, Rolf. The boy is fragile and would not stand some of the treatment that we mete out at times if there is a reason and it is truthful. I will understand, after all, they are both grieving.'

'I think that we must make haste before they lose more blood. The boy is young and could recover, but the old warrior might not,' came Rolf's reply.

'Aye, you're right, Rolf. We can blood let at a later date if necessary, and I feel that Godfrey is loyal even if his loyalty is split two ways.'

'Yes, he certainly loved his old friend,' Rolf replied as he set his mount back towards Alder-Sea manor.

The small band were soon making way back along with their prisoner and the wounded up on their horses and were returning to the manor. Gilbert studied the face of Guy as he was held firm in his arms making sure that he would not fall as they travelled back.

Guy had lost his hat, and he noticed the golden curls had been washed clean and were the colour of spun gold, his golden lashes lay long and thick upon his cheeks. *By the Holy Mother,* he thought, *this child has the looks of a beautiful angel. He could be taken for a maiden.* Gilbert had never seen the like. The child's beauty had stirred his senses. He must pull himself together before he arrived back at Alder-sea. It was as if his wits had gone abegging. What had gotten into him? He had seen beautiful women before, and this boy was as beautiful as any maiden. He felt for the boy. Perhaps it was because he knew that Guy had suffered a great loss when he lost George. That was it. He was feeling sorry for the boy especially as it was possible that he would lose his other champion, Godfrey.

He was still puzzled though as to what business had taken Godfrey and Guy into the forest on their own, and he had only seen one horse. *Now why was that?* he thought. He would have to wait to get answers; however, answers he would have if they recovered from their injuries. He needed to clear up this mystery.

Although he could not understand why he thought of the child so much, he vowed he would take care of him, and if he found a suitable maid to take for a wife, Guy would make an ideal page for her in his household.

He didn't want to ride too fast in case the movement of galloping was detrimental to the boy. They would soon reach the castle grounds, and a physician would be able to assess the damage to both Guy and Godfrey.

God knows the villagers were already in mourning for George, and he hoped that they wouldn't need to for Godfrey. Perhaps there was family that would grieve for Guy if he didn't make it. If it was left to Gilbert, he would make sure he had the best care possible. After all, they could make some strong potions with the herbs that were grown in the garden. Hadn't Guy already pointed out that the garden patch was important and needed to be kept?

Gilbert's mind went back to the day they were looking at the land behind the dovecote. Guy's clear, concise way he made it known that garden of herbs must not be touched. As a serf, he had no say. He also remembered how George had quickly turned the speech towards a reason. Why would he allow a serf to speak up when it wasn't his place to have an opinion? And at the stables, the horse, Star, had broken loose and appeared to be familiar as if the boy was his master. He had given these incidents little thought at the time, but they were now beginning push forward in his mind. He needed to have answers to these incidents from Godfrey and Guy, God willing. Yes, he would wait until they had recovered enough. Gilbert needed to understand the reason why.

The little band of horses rode into the courtyard of the Alder-Sea in a sober mood, calling for the help of the soldiers. He at once dispatched one in search of the physician to attend to the two friends. *Yes, friends*, he thought. They had been but strangers less than three weeks ago. He found that the two people were now quite important to him. God knows he had dispatched many a stranger on the battlefield without a regret. Now he was heartily sick with death and the war. He hoped that Godfrey and Guy would recover.

Whatever their plan had been, he was sure they could overcome it. Gilbert needed to know why they were so deep in the wood when he thought he had warned Guy, but they were both together. It was a puzzle. It could be that Guy had wandered off in his distress, and Godfrey had been forced to ride out and find him. *Underneath*, he thought, *there might be a deeper reason*. He would try to find out and understand the reasoning when both Guy and Godfrey were on the mend.

Godfrey's horse was handed to the groom with the rest of the horses. The groom was not party to George's plan, and he noticed the bundle hanging from Godfrey's horse's saddle. Glancing around him, he took the bundle and hid it out of sight in the stable. He blessed the Holy Mother that Lord Gilbert and the other knights had not thought fit to examine it. Whatever it was, Lord Godfrey would have his reasons. He would quietly speak with Percival when it was safe to do so.

As Gilbert handed the child to the awaiting soldier, he noticed how pale he was.

'Be careful with him. Place him in Lord George's solar along with Godfrey. I will get help to clean the wounds up,' he said with a nod of his head. Following the soldiers carrying the two wounded people to the solar, he was anxious for the physician to attend them.

He also needed someone to attend and help. That would be a task for Wulf. He could attend and help to run errands with requests from the physician. He at once dispatched another passing soldier to urge the physician Edgar to hurry and attend the wounded and to alert Wulf that he was required. He watched that Godfrey was placed carefully on the bed and that Guy was made comfortable on the pallet by the wall. The fire was quickly lit by a soldier and the water can hung on the hook to heat fresh cloths were put ready for Edgar to use.

Wulf knocked on the solar door, 'My Lord Gilbert has sent for me, sir,' he addressed Rolf as he opened the door.

'Come in, boy,' Rolf answered.

Percival, the castle reeve, was hot on Wulf's heels. 'You needed me, my Lord Gilbert?'

'Yes, Percival, Guy and Godfrey were attacked in the forest. It was a good thing that we were out with soldiers hunting a sighting of renegades that had been reported. We saved them further harm. I need you to assist in undressing Godfrey so that his wounds can be attended to, and you, Wulf, if you could do the same for Guy but be gentle with him?' The look on Wulf's face astounded Gilbert. 'Well, boy, what are you standing there for with that stupid look on your face?' he roared.

'But sir,' he stuttered, his face red as he looked on the figure of Guy lying still and almost lifeless.

'Come, boy, time is of the essence. Do you want Guy to die?' he asked, walking over to Guy and gently began to remove his tunic suddenly stopping as he saw the rough binding across his chest. 'By the Holy Mother, has he been injured already? Has he some strange malady that he needs to dress so?' he asked.

At this, Percival stepped in, 'My Lord Gilbert, perhaps you need the help of a maid. I'm sure Enid would be of help.'

'The boy needs to toughen up,' Gilbert spit out, more because he was anxious than angry. He quickly took a knife and cut the binding away, stepping away in astonishment.

'My Lord Gilbert,' Percival had tried to stop him. Too late, the small breasts of what was unmistakably a maiden burst out of its wrapping.

The look of amazement and anger on his face as he barked out, 'Wulf, fetch Enid and not a word of what you have just seen, understand?'

'Yes, my lord,' came Wulf's answer, his face red with embarrassment as he scuttled away to do his master's bidding. Quickly covering Guy with the nearest garment, all the feelings of curiosity and being drawn towards the child bubbled up into reality. He now knew why he had been drawn to this slender child. Why?! Did they think he was an animal that would deflower any maiden that he came upon? He would not be so base, why was she sharing George's solar? He felt anger at the thought she was just a maiden child, surely George was a godly person. By God he would get to the truth of the matter. They had sought to hoodwink and mistrust him, yes, he would have the truth. It was likely there would be a reason, and he needed to find what. And he was aware that he could not do this until Guy and Godfrey were healing. What was Guy thinking! Who was she and of what name?

At that moment, Enid entered.

'Wash the child and find a shift for her. Once you have done that, you are excused working in the kitchen. You will now be the personal lady-in-waiting until further notice and will not leave her side, understand?' his grey eyes appearing to spit shards of steel as they glared at her in anger.

Hounds teeth, Enid thought, she hadn't realised that Lord Gilbert could be so angry. 'Yes, my lord,' Enid answered as she looked for warm water and a bowl, then looking at the door.

'Just one more question, girl. Did you know Guy was a maiden?' he asked, fixing her with his grey eyes that glowered at her. Enid was verily shaking in her shoes; she could not see any good reason in her being untruthful to her Lord Gilbert because she was sure now the truth would out and that the Lady Gytha would realise that she had no other option than tell the truth.

Besides, she realised herself that Lord Gilbert would not hurt either of them. He was angry, and when all was explained to him, he would understand. What if Godfrey or Gytha did not recover? There would be many who would sing both Godfrey's praises and Gytha's. Enid began to undress her friend and gently wash her. She too wanted to cry as she saw the wound her on friend's head. Before leaving, Gilbert had repositioned the screen between the injured knight and the maid and was just about to leave the solar as the physician arrived to attend them.

Gilbert said with in a gentler tone to his voice, 'We have lost Lord George. We don't want to lose this old warrior or the maiden. Make sure you stay with them and do everything you can to repair the damage that has been done by the scoundrels we sent to their maker. This village does not need more sorrow. Godfrey is well-loved and respected by all including myself.'

The physician, Edgar, nodded his head and at once set to work on Godfrey, removing the arrow and firing the wound. His wounds were dressed and covered with balm that had been made from the herbs grown in the garden. They had made a potion to put on a linen cloth and applied it to his nose to help Godfrey to sleep. Sleep was a good healer. The stab wound had missed any vital organs and was just a clean cut which he stitched and covered with a cloth covered once more in the special balm.

Percival cleaned him and dressed him in night garments and made him comfortable. Sitting down at the side of him, he prepared to stand guard over him. He had also located the coins in Godfrey's clothing, carefully removing them when no one was watching. He would keep them safe until his Lord Godfrey could have them back. He had observed Godfrey leave the confines of the castle and had thought the old warrior had a purposeful look upon his face as he rode out on a larger mount than normal. He had felt that something was afoot as soon as George had dressed Gytha as a serf, a lad at that.

Edgar had then quickly turned his attention to Gytha. He addressed Enid, 'She is young and strong. It is a nasty bump, get me some more warm water, and we will clean the wound.'

'There you are, sir,' Enid said.

Once he had cleaned the wound, he said, 'We must stitch it. She is unconscious and won't feel it.' Enid watched him carefully stitch the wound making the stitches as small as he could. He maintained it would not scar as much. Her hair, when grown, would cover it. Gytha made a small moan but did not wake.

'Thank the holy saints,' Enid whispered.

'She will perhaps sleep but will need this potion on a cloth if she wakes. I will just report their condition to Lord Gilbert, then I will be back. We will both need rest at some time. And hopefully tomorrow they will show signs of improvement. Watch over our Lady Gytha, and you,

Percival, watch Godfrey carefully for any change in condition. The next few hours will be critical and should show which way he will go,' the physician told them gravely, looking down at the elderly knight. He, like Godfrey, had resided at Alder-Sea all his life. He liked and respected the old knight, and now everything could change in only a few hours. Sighing, he left the room in search of Gilbert.

As Edgar left them, Percival turned to Enid and said, 'Don't worry, Lord Gilbert is a fair man. If we tell the truth, I'm sure he will understand why our Lord George chose to protect Gytha from being hurt.'

'Yes, I think our Lord Gilbert is a fair man, and he will deal carefully with the situation. He already respects Godfrey, and when he gets to know our Lady Gytha, he will like her too,' Enid replied.

They were both happy to lose sleep and watch over their two good friends. Everything else would wait until Gilbert could have speech with the wounded members of the Castle Alder-sea. They both looked at their patients and slipped into deep thought. Yes, Enid thought, she was sure that Lord Gilbert would deal fairly with her friends.

It seemed a long time before the physician returned to sit with them. A soldier came with him carrying an extra pallet for one of them to sleep. Enid insisted that it should be Percival, and they could take turns. She would be last being the youngest and would not need the sleep as much.

And it gave her a little more satisfaction that Wally would have to do a little more work now that she was to work inside with her Lady Gytha. She was happy to be with her friend. How she wished she hadn't been ordered by her grandfather to leave. Enid was sure that Lord Gilbert would take care of her. She didn't dare to tell anyone that Gytha liked him. *Truth be told,* Enid thought, *not just like, she is half in love with her Lord Gilbert*. Enid had seen how she looked when she had revealed her secret. Her lips said like but her eyes said love. Enid remembered the solar that was now occupied by Lord Gilbert. Perhaps one day her friend would move back into it.

Enid sat and watched her old friend, and as she became restless, she gave her some potion on the cloth and gently held it over her nose to help her drift back into a healing sleep. This was repeated with Godfrey so that he would not feel the pain.

Enid and Percival were sent to get a little sleep when morning came. The physician was refreshed and sitting with his patients. Wulf returned to help, along with the seamstress. Godfrey had a fever and cold flannels were applied to his head to help sooth it. While they were attending to the patients, they sat and talked. Edgar told them to call him by his name as it was easier, and they talked in whispers as not to disturb the patients.

Now Gytha was sleeping peacefully, and Edgar was sure that she would recover. With Godfrey, it was different. The old warrior was not as strong as he used to be, and the fever had not helped. They had reduced the fever, but his condition still worried Edgar. Checking the wound, he saw there was no infection. It was just the fever that he was concerned about. Hopefully, Godfrey would be strong enough to overcome it.

Gilbert came after breaking his fast. He couldn't stay away too long. He had tried, and inside he was still angry that they had not trusted him with the child's identity. He would not push the serfs for answers. He would wait for the maid and Godfrey to explain to him why they had felt it necessary to deceive him. His main worry was he wanted both of them to recover. He realised he had feelings for the maid. He had recognised the attraction when he thought he was Guy and could not understand it. Yes, he wanted a maid, the maid with the beautiful lavender blue eyes. It was those eyes that had captured his heart.

He realised he would have to think and tread carefully before he showed his hand. He now knew this maid would be his destiny. How Godfrey and the maid would feel was not yet known. All Gilbert wanted was to see them both well again. He would wait but he must have speech with both. He hoped the girl was still a maid and had not been spoiled by anyone. He wanted her but in marriage, and he didn't even know her name, he just knew it could not be Guy.

'How is Godfrey this morning?' he asked Edgar.

'His fever is over. I have great hopes of him recovering, my lord, but only time will tell,' he replied.

'And the maid, will she recover?'

'We will keep both sedated for a couple of days, then most of the pain will have subdued.'

'That's what I wanted to hear,' Gilbert answered.

'It would be prudent to give them a few more days to recover before you perhaps talk to them. It would not do to reinstate pain too soon, my lord,' Edgar said hopefully to Gilbert.

'I understand. I will need to know why, my curiosity is getting the better of me, but I will wait, my friend. Besides, we have the prisoner to try. He and his two comrades injured Guy and Godfrey, and he must pay for the attack on two innocent people.'

Gytha was the first to recover and was still a little weary and her head hurt. Enid was overjoyed and at once sent the serf that was in the corridor to fetch and carry to the kitchens for some chicken broth. Once he was back, she gently coaxed her to swallow some of the soup and gave her a wash behind the screen.

Edgar at once asked, 'Is your head still hurting, my lady?'

'Yes,' she whispered.

'Then perhaps you should sleep some more. If I give you a little more potion to help you sleep, I'm sure you will be able to get up and sit in the chair to rest tomorrow. Enid or Lisa, the seamstress, will sit with you throughout the night so you are always watched over, my lady, and you also have myself and Percival in attendance to watch over our Lord Godfrey.'

Gytha suddenly looked stricken, 'Is my Lord Godfrey alright?' she whispered. 'I couldn't bear if…' and her voice petered off as she thought of her grandfather. Godfrey was all she had left.

'Come, my lady, have a little more potion. I swear you will feel much better tomorrow when you have had more rest.' Lifting the cup to her lips, she drank the potion. Enid sat and held her hand as she drifted away to sleep once more to take away her worries.

Gilbert visited the solar again to see if there was any improvement and was pleased that the maid had recovered enough to take some broth. He was now sure she would recover, and he would be able to gaze into those bewitching eyes.

'What about Godfrey?' he asked Edgar.

'Yes, my lord. The Wiley old knight is responding. The fever has abated, and I feel he will be awakened by tomorrow.'

'Well, I'll leave both of them in your good hands. I can tell you, Edgar, I am much relieved.'

'I will advise you when Godfrey wakes, my lord,' came Edgar's reply. With a nod of his head and another glance at the maid, he left, closing the door quietly behind him. Why, she was beautiful, he thought. His heart was sore. He needed to know why she shared George's solar; only then would he feel happy.

Enid sat and watched Gytha as she slept peacefully. She was relieved it would only be a matter of time and her lady would be recovered fully. Although she did not envy the speech that was to take place with Gilbert, she was sure he would forgive her duplicity but not before he had shown her his displeasure.

Turning her attention to Godfrey as she heard his slight moan, Enid stood and walked to stand behind Percival as he watched Godfrey waking from his sleep.

Percival said, 'Don't struggle to move, my lord. I will alert Edgar. He has just gone to his rooms for more potion that has been mixed.' Opening the door, he sent the awaiting serf that was standing there to fetch a bowl of some broth. He could take a little, then Edgar would give him another draft of potion to help the old warrior to rest more. Percival and Enid were pleased to see that he was returning to the land of the living, happy that their Lady Gytha would not have to grieve more.

The serf was soon back, and Percival lifted Godfrey's head, making sure that he did not disturb the healing wounds so that he could swallow the warm broth that Enid carefully spooned into his mouth. Wulf was standing by with a cloth to wipe his chin if necessary.

Looking up at Percival, Godfrey whispered, 'My Lord Gilbert.'

'Shush, save your breath, my lord. Gilbert is only interested in you recovering. Yes, he was angry that you were out in the forest with my lady, and I think he is somewhat hurt over the duplicity practiced. I'm afraid my

Lord Gilbert's bark is worse than his bite, although he only wishes to see your recovery at the moment.'

Edgar walked into the solar, his face beaming, 'Well, my Lord Godfrey, we have you back in the land of the living. I'm certain our Lord Gilbert will be much relieved. Let me look at your wounds to make sure they are healing well, then Percival will wash you and a little more sleep is what I recommend. The pain by then will be less, my old friend.'

Percival filled the bowl with warm water that Enid had kept heated over the fire. Enid moved around the screen as Percival prepared to wash Godfrey.

Clutching Percival's hand, he asked in a low voice, 'How fares my lady?'

'My Lady Gytha is well on the way to recovering. She also awoke earlier and took some broth and is sleeping like a baby, my lord. So, let's concentrate on you for the time being. My lady is in the good hands of Enid who has been elevated to her lady-in-waiting.'

'Does he know who he is dealing with?'

'No, my lord, just that she's a maid. I'll wager he will have worked it out, so no good will come out of untruths. We all know you acted in good faith.' Godfrey sunk back on his cushions, exhaustion caused by the effort of speech. 'Now, my lord, be quiet while I wash you then you can sleep more and regain your strength once more.'

Looking at Percival, he gave him a wry smile. 'It was my Lord George's orders that I acted on. I have twice tried to carry out his wishes, but it seems that it wasn't meant to be. Now it is in the hands of God as to the outcome. I hope my Lord Gilbert is an understanding man,' Godfrey said wearily as Percival held the cup of elixir to help sleep overcome his mind for a short while longer.

Chapter 9

Gilbert summoned Gunter and Rolf. 'It's time we spoke to our Norman prisoner. He left William's army with one thought, to besmirch the Norman name and make out that we are all just intent on killing, sacking and raping their women. It's no wonder that the Saxons view us with mistrust. This is not the legacy that William dreams of. He wants peace and for England to unite and thrive under his rule.'

'Aye, you're right, Gilbert,' Gunter said.

'Well, we need to bring the prisoner in to interrogate him. There might be more hiding in the forest. If there are, we need to flush them out, but first bring the prisoner in, and we can get to the bottom of what happened. He nearly killed one of our knights along with a maiden.'

Rolf looked at Gilbert, curiosity all over his face. 'Maiden, which maiden?' he asked.

'Well, that is what I need to find out. Guy is a maiden. It appears that most here knew except us.'

'By the saints, what mischief was afoot,' Gunter added.

'I know they should have told me, but I do understand they would be loyal to Lord George. I would have protected them whatever their status.'

'I'll instruct the guard to bring up the prisoner. I'll be quite interested myself in what he has to say, Gilbert.'

At this, Rolf marched away eager to find out what himself, Gunter and Gilbert would discover. He himself liked Lord George, and funnily enough, he had felt sorry for Guy thinking that he was feminine. Yes, he thought, *for a boy he cut a sorry figure,* but now he understood. He too wondered who the maiden was. *Curiosity killed the cat,* he thought.

He quickly dispatched two soldiers to escort the prisoner to the small room they used for disputes and interrogating prisoners. This could be a matter of life or death for the prisoner for although Gilbert could be benign, he could also mete out harsh punishment to threats against his home or people that transgressed against anyone under his protection, and Godfrey and Guy were.

Soon the soldiers marched into the guardhouse, not bothering to release the chains upon the hands of the prisoner. They wrinkled their noses at the stench of his body. It was clear that it had been quite a long time since he had bathed.

He too was a Norman. One that had fled his duty that had brought him to England with William and for that alone he could lose his life. He had helped to flame the anger of the Saxons by burning and sacking unprotected manors, and this had not helped William's cause.

Walking between the two guards, he cut a sorry figure. Most Normans preferred to be clean shaven whilst the Saxons favoured beards. This Norman soldier had not taken care of his appearance. It was obvious that he had been on the run and hiding in the forest. There were many hidden caves in the forest, and as yet, they hadn't searched them out. They could see that this would be a mission that Gilbert would make one of his priorities.

The prisoner was led into the small room where they found Gilbert sitting in a large wooden chair. The Norman soldier pulled himself up to show that he wasn't afraid of the man in front of him. Surely, he would see that he was a Norman, and it had only been a couple of Saxon rabbles that they had shot at. Where he a fellow Norman had killed two of their own countrymen. Gilbert's grey eyes settled on the prisoner. They were like grey shards of silver looking into the depths of the Norman renegade's mind. Because Gilbert didn't speak for a few moments, he began to squirm under the scrutiny of his fellow Norman.

'State your name,' Gilbert said in a quiet voice.

'Kurt Ludwig. I'm a member of King William's army and should not have been shackled in this way.'

'You are a soldier late of William's army. No soldier of William's would be as badly kept as yourself nor would they attack a defenceless elderly knight and a young person, almost killing them.'

The Norman sneered. 'They were only Saxons. They would have been better dead, what care I about them?'

Gilbert's face changed. 'We did not come to England to kill without a reason, and you are a deserter and a coward,' he said, a ferocious look upon his face.

Gunter spoke up, 'How many more of you cowardly deserters are in the forest? You are the band that we were warned about. You have been burning villages, killing men, women and children, whatever their age.'

'I'm a Norman and so were my comrades you killed in the attack on us. We were your comrades in arms. Surely, we were more important than Saxon rabble?'

'Those rabble as you called them are my villagers, and no one but I can punish them. They have not committed any crimes. You have not only committed crimes against innocent people, but you have also committed a crime against King William, and I, Gilbert Bayeux, have sworn to uphold his law. So, how many more of you cowardly wretches are there hidden in the forest?' he grated out.

'Answer your Lord Gilbert now,' Gunter growled.

'Why should I? He's a Norman the same as I. We are no different, he and I,' the Norman sneered. 'We have both killed the Saxon rabble.'

Gilbert stood as if to turn to Gunter. Moving liked lightning, he changed his course, his fist smashing into the Norman deserter's face knocking his front teeth out.

'Perhaps that will loosen your tongue, and if I have killed Saxons it has been in fair combat in defence of our king,' rasped Gilbert.

'Never!' the Norman soldier threw back.

'Take him back to the guard house where he can contemplate the rope that is waiting for him. I swear we will route out your comrades, and they will get the same fate. Neither we nor William hold with attacking people that are going about their own business peacefully. We did not come to England to kill or ransack innocent people's homes.'

Gunter instantly moved to instruct the soldiers to remove the prisoner from the room. Noticing that Gilbert was in a ferocious mood, he would not like to cross him today. He would make sure that himself and Rolf were gainfully employed in carrying out Gilbert's instructions for the rest of the day.

Gilbert felt as if he could have cheerfully strangled the Norman there and then. He could have killed Guy, he now realised. Why he was so angry? He had fallen in love with the maid who had lavender blue eyes, even when he thought she was a boy. It must have been instinct. He had looked upon the face of Guy as he lay unconscious and the maid's beauty was obvious. That must have been why he always looked away when Gilbert had gazed at her face. He needed to tread carefully. He was not sure how old she was. What Gilbert did know was that this maid was destined to grace his bed. He would not rest until he knew the fair maid's name.

He would take a small band of soldiers out and search the caves within the forest and rid Alder-Sea lands of the threat to his villagers and any person travelling in or out. Visitors to their land would have safe passage. Making his way back to the main hall in search of Gunter and Rolf, he found them just entering the hall.

When Gilbert outlined what he wanted to do, the two knights said they would choose a band of their best fighters among the soldiers to search and clear the woods and caves of any threat within the woods and would not leave a cave unsearched until they were sure that the forest was clear of any deserters or groups of Saxon bandits.

'I suggest you, Gilbert, find out who the maid is. I went to check on the old warrior, and I gazed on the maid's face. I thought as Guy the child was pretty. I wonder if she is still a maid,' he laughed at Gilbert.

Suddenly, he realised that he did not find his jest funny. 'Careful how you speak of the maid, my friend. I have plans for her,' he warned Gunter with a scowl on his face, making his friends aware that it was time they made a swift exit.

Gunter could only reply, 'Oh! In that case, I will go about my business and clear them woods just in case you have a mind to hit me. I wouldn't like to be at the end of your fist. I wouldn't be as pretty.' He said this quickly, saluting Gilbert as they went.

Rolf threw in, 'We had better make ourselves scarce, our friend Gilbert is not in a good mood. We will return when your mood is sweeter,' he jested, making a fast exit.

Another three days passed before Gilbert had time to visit Edgar the physician. He now knew that the maid and Godfrey were out of bed and recovering. He decided they were out of danger and needed to counsel himself on how to approach this problem. He had no wish to upset Godfrey. The old knight was weak. Gilbert also knew that he would have to be careful in how he questioned the maid. He needed answers before he made his intentions clear.

It would not be long before he had to join William in the north to quell the uprising of Saxons in that area. He would like everything in place before he left to join William. God willing, he would not be away for long. Now he had found this maid, if he had the right answers to his questions, he was sure he would have no appetite to leave her after looking into her beautiful eyes. He would have sworn this maiden had bewitched him even when he had thought she was not a maiden.

After great thought, Gilbert decided to go with Gunter to help clear the woods, leaving Rolf in charge at the manor. After a complete week, he had another three of the band of deserters in the guard house. He was happy that there would be safe passage through the forest now. They would question these other prisoners at the end of the week, and they would be hanged outside of the manor away from the delicate eyes of the ladies within the village.

Retiring to bed, he decided he would see the maid tomorrow. That way he could have their stories separate, and he would not have to embarrass the maid in front of Godfrey. He would then speak to Godfrey and hopefully put his plan to the old knight if he had to. Gilbert did not catch a lot of sleep that night as his mind kept going over different scenarios to his problem, his heart dictating the endings, some good, some bad.

He felt as if he had only just gone to sleep when Enid was at the door with his breakfast. He hastily dressed and opened the door.

'Your breakfast, my lord.'

'Thank you. Would you just put a light to the fire for me? I've overslept this morning.'

'Yes, my lord,' Enid answered busying herself in building the fire.

'Tell me, Enid. You know the maid that was known as Guy. Is she of good character?'

'Why, yes, my lord! She is my friend.'

'Are you aware if she is of good family and chaste?' he hesitated over the last part of the question.

'Why, of course, my lord. Will that be all?' she asked, her cheeks now crimson.

Realising that he had embarrassed the girl he said, 'You may go about your business, Enid, and thank you.'

Sitting and looking at the bread and meat that she had brought in for him to break his fast, he made no attempt to eat, just stared moodily into the fire. What if she had been telling him what he needed to hear and not the truth? How would he then recognise deceit? They were all loyal to Lord George. They still had to know Lord Gilbert to form their loyalty to him. Sighing, he reached for his goblet of ale and drank. He would give them time to break their fast, and he would send Wulf to see if they were up and about, and then he would have speech with each one of them before he decided on the next step.

Wulf was soon back reporting that the maid was now up and sitting with Godfrey. Enid had just gone in to relieve the seamstress who had been sitting with her lady, after slipping to the kitchens to fetch her breakfast. Wally was busy and asked her to drop off her Lord Gilbert's food to break his fast. Now Enid wished that she had gone straight to relieve her friend the seamstress and broke her fast with them.

Godfrey had moved to his own solar and returned to sit with his Lady Rowlands to be on hand if Gilbert saw fit to send for them. They would then be able to be together, and he thought he could persuade Gilbert that it was his and

George's fault that her identity had been kept secret to ensure that his lady was safe. It 'twas no matter how he would be punished. He needed to know his lady was safe. His lady was too genteel to take harsh punishment and harsh words. He was sorry it had come to this and felt that he had let his Lord George down. If he had still been young and strong, he would have been strong enough to fight off the villains that had attacked them and succeed in his task.

They were both sitting quietly by the fire when Enid opened the door to let Wulf in, 'Pardon, my lady, Lord Gilbert would like to know if you are recovered enough for you to visit him in the small room used to settle disputes.' She stood up, looking taller dressed in the lavender blue gown that Enid had helped her to put on. Her golden hair was shining like gold in tight curls looking more like an angel than ever.

'Yes, I am feeling quite well, Wulf, and will come to the dispute room in a few minutes. You can tell my Lord Gilbert.'

'I too will accompany my lady,' Godfrey informed him.

'My Lord Gilbert asked me to advise you that he would see you, my lord, after and that I will escort my lady back, sir.' It was obvious that Wulf was embarrassed to be passing on this message. He liked and respected Godfrey enormously and would have done anything to spare his feelings.

The young maid with the lavender blue eyes stood and held up her hand, 'Don't worry on my account, Godfrey. I am a match for my Lord Gilbert. I am my father's daughter and George's granddaughter; he holds no fears for me. Besides, I still have you and will ensure that you will be always at my side, my lord.' Picking up a copper plate, the maid checked her appearance and was pleased that she had regained a little colour. 'Lead on, Wulf, we will soon have this audience completed with our lord.' Wulf turned and the maid followed. If Gytha felt any trepidation, she did not show it.

When they entered the small anti-room, Gilbert was sitting on the large wooden chair that her grandfather had always sat on in the past when he was setting judgement on a dispute. The only thing missing was the village priest who would normally attend such sessions. Her Lord Gilbert must have felt it was not necessary. If he thought because she was a maid she would be cowed, he was quite wrong. The anger that he had thought it necessary to bring her to this room bubbled up inside her. He was the enemy, not her.

'You wished to see me, my lord,' launching straight into speech before he could. Gilbert looked up in surprise. She had caught him off guard. Looking directly into those lavender blue eyes, his heart was instantly smote.

It took him a few seconds before he broke into speech, 'Yes, I have some questions to ask you. Can you tell me why you, a young maiden of tender age, resided in Lord George's solar? Also, I need to know that you are still a maiden and have not been besmirched.'

Her eyes opened wide with shock at the questions asked. He, the enemy, was accusing her grandfather of unspeakable crimes. Lord George was her beloved grandfather and had only been bent on protecting her honour from the Normans that had pillaged and raped the maidens in the many manors. Who did Gilbert the Norman knight think he was? This manor had been built by her great grandfather before George, and he, Gilbert was the enemy and had no right to be questioning her. Hadn't her father died trying to be loyal to their elected king Harold and to protect the rights of the Saxon noblemen? It could have even been his sword that had cut down her father and uncle.

'How dare you ask me such questions! You who have no right to be here. You have taken over our lands, you that have come to our shores for gain.'

'I dare because I am your overlord, and you would do well to remember that. Now, answer my question,' came his outraged answer as he half rose from his chair.

'How dare you say such things about Lord George? He who only made sure that you did not dishonour me as most of your fellow invaders have at other manors.'

'Why would Lord George be bothered to protect a young maiden from the advances of mere men?' came his reply as he fixed his gaze on her face hungrily. Thinking, *mere men that had been at war for over a year and a half. Men that were missing the company of maids, and who could blame them if the maids were willing.* He would never have taken a maiden against her will.

'Why?' she asked scathingly. Once started, it was hard to stop and reason why.

'Tell me, are you of good family?'

'Everyone is born of good family, my lord. It is what you make of yourself that matters,' she spat out.

'If you won't answer because you feel above the serfs in this manor, tell your name, maid,' he leant forward in his chair and fixed her with a steely gaze. *My God, this maid had spirit. It would be interesting to tame her.* He knew he was completely lost to her charms.

Staring back, her eyes unwavering as they fixed on his, she answered, 'I have more rights to be here than you, Gilbert Bayeux. My name is Lady Gytha Rowlands. My Lord George watched over me because I am his granddaughter, and you asked if I had been besmirched, the very thing that he made sure did not happen to me.

You outrage me, sir. Knights like you and your soldiers have raped young girls like me and murdered their families. Do you blame my grandfather for protecting me?'

'My soldiers or my friends have not raped or murdered anyone. We have fought a fair war against good Saxons who died bravely in defence of their beliefs.'

Gytha stamped her small foot and cried, 'Tush, a truthful Norman, never.'

Gilbert jumped in his own defence stating, 'I speak truth, lady. I did not come to England for gain. I'm here to see England flourish under its rightful ruler in peace and prosperity.' Gytha saw a strange look on his face she realised she had judged him wrongly, and her barb had hit home. All Normans were not the same. Had he not been kind to her when he thought her a lowly boy?

'I'm sorry, I have been rude, my lord. I must guard my tongue. I realise you are different,' she said as a halting apology. This had been hard for Gytha to admit to herself, and Gilbert immediately sensed a change in her, grasping the olive branch and turning it to his advantage.

'I am sorry too that we spoke in anger. I had to ask you these questions. How old are you, Lady Gytha?'

Stretching up to her full five foot two she answered, 'I will be seventeen in a few weeks, not that it should concern you, my lord.'

'That is where you are wrong, sweet lady. As overlord to Alder-Sea it meant you became my ward when I was granted these lands.' His voice was low and had a strange tone that sent a shiver of anticipation through her bones, making her stomach flutter.

'Your ward?'

'Yes, my lady, so would you feel more comfortable if you are to be reinstated once more as lady of this manor?

You who kneeled at my feet and swore loyalty to me as the young boy Guy?'

'It would only be my natural right, my lord,' came Gytha's answer as her glance did not waver.

'I see, sweet lady. You may return to your solar. I will decide what we can do about this after I have discovered what our Lord Godfrey's role has been in this, as he too swore loyalty to myself. I'm not sure that acting this way was loyal.' He watched her face as he made this statement. He realised that Godfrey now was her weak point. She immediately threw herself at his feet. Her gown was like a cloud of blue silk billowing around her.

'Please, my lord, don't punish my Lord Godfrey. He is old and frail, and he was only obeying my grandfather's wishes. I will do anything. Please don't punish him,' she said as she raised her blue eyes to him that were now swimming with unshed tears.

The breath caught in his throat. Never had he seen a maiden more beautiful. He wanted to tell her not to be affeered, as he pushed the words back. He wanted to say, 'I will punish neither of you. I love you, Gytha.' He now realised why it had been so easy for them to call her Guy. He needed to keep his feelings to himself until he had speech with Godfrey.

'Well, sweet lady, I have indeed a solution to our problem. I need to have speech with Godfrey first. Dry those pretty eyes, and you can return to your solar for the time being; however, I expect you to dine in the main hall tonight with me. I will guide you myself, so stay in your solar until I come for you.'

'Yes, my lord,' came her answer. Why was he using endearments to her when he spoke? He had appeared to be angry to start with and had quickly changed to being amenable, and Gytha couldn't quite understand.

'Just one more thing, my lady. I feel that you have not yet lain down your arms. You are still fighting your destiny. Something that Saxons and Normans need to do to bring peace to our lives together in England. Think about it, my lady, would you fight me for the rest of our life?' he asked of her.

Her words came in a whisper, 'Our lives, my lord?'

'Aye, our lives.' There seemed to be a promise of something in his words and the way he looked at her and for the life of her she didn't quite understand what. Only that she had a slight excited feeling. Yes, she felt as if something good would happen, but how, what? she questioned herself. Her mind turned back to her Lord Godfrey. She would protect him with her own life. She had lost Grandfather, and she could not stand to lose his old friend Godfrey too. He had always been around her, protecting her, when her father or grandfather had not been present to do so.

Walking to the door, he called Wulf in, 'You may escort the Lady Gytha back to her solar and inform Lord Godfrey that I await him here.'

'Yes, my lord,' came Wulf's answer, somewhat relieved that his Lady Gytha was no worse for wear after her interview.

Wulf was quiet as they walked back to the solar. It seemed like a lifetime away that they had played in the woods together, a small group of innocent children slaying dragons and rescuing fair maidens. Gytha had grown up now and had been his master's granddaughter and as such, he needed to respect her position. For once, he was lost for words. He never had to watch what he said when they were children, and he found it hard now. He was in Lord Gilbert's employ now, and he needed to know his place.

Gytha stopped as she opened the door and thanked Wulf for walking back to the solar with her.

'I need to escort my Lord Godfrey back, my lady,' so entering the solar he lost no time in giving his message to Godfrey.

'Of course, Wulf.'

'Thank you, sir,' the young lad said with a smile. It was like being family even though he had been a serf.

'Are you alright, my lady?' Godfrey asked of Gytha, even though he had been sure that his Lord Gilbert would not have treated her harshly; however, he wasn't sure how he himself would fare.

Walking at the side of Wulf, he too was quiet. Perhaps Gilbert would not be as lenient with him, although he had found Gilbert to be a fair man. Godfrey hoped once he explained, he wouldn't be too harsh with him. If not, he would accept his punishment with pride. He too loved Lady Gytha. Godfrey had always felt part of the family and not just one of George's knights.

Walking into the anti-room, he too found Gilbert sitting on the huge wooden chair. He also had placed a chair for Godfrey to sit.

'How are you, my old friend? Sufficiently recovered after your ordeal in the woods, I hope?' he asked the old knight.

'Yes, my lord. I'm sorry we felt that we needed to keep the Lady Gytha's identity from you. There have been so many attacks on the maidens within different manors that my Lord George felt Gytha would fare better if she was a boy.'

'Why, Godfrey?'

'We neither had any idea what sort of person you would be.'

'And now, my lord, what do you feel now?' came Gilbert's quiet question.

'That you are a fair and compassionate man. I feel that you have chosen not to punish my lady and for that I am grateful.'

'I see,' were Gilbert's only words.

'You must deal with me as you wish, and I thank you for dealing with Gytha how you have. She is young and has always appeared to trust you despite the deception on this matter. I fear she had more common sense than me or George.'

'I could do no other as Guy. She was dear to me. Do you understand, Godfrey? I could not understand myself in the beginning.'

'Yes, my lord, I believe I do. Many times I saw the way you looked and thought you had realised that Guy was a maiden. Now I understand.'

'Our lady Gytha fears that I will punish you, but I know you were only doing George's bidding. Whatever you did, you would have been disloyal to one of us, it was natural that you were loyal to George.'

'Thank you for being understanding, my Lord Gilbert.'

'I would not punish you, Godfrey, but I would like your help.'

'Help, my lord? Of course, and I feel that I know what you need help with. You love our Lady Gytha?'

'Yes, Godfrey I do. She would like to be reinstated as the lady of this manor and the only way is to become my wife. I promise I would love and cherish her for the rest of my life. I'm fearful that she would not come willingly without your help.'

'I can tell you, my lord, with the trust of a young person she herself thought you would look after her as well as looking after myself and George. My lord didn't want to take any chances, although he himself thought you a fair man,' Godfrey explained with a smile.

'Then you will help me with my heart's desire and help the young maiden understand I wish her no harm, and that I will cherish her for the rest of her life? I know I will be called to arms again soon and would wed the sweet lady before going to the north to serve William.'

'Yes, my Lord Gilbert, I would see my lady at peace and safe in your care before I join my Lord George in the hereafter.'

'It will be a long time before that happens, Godfrey. I will make you her protector whilst I'm away and leave my friend Gunter behind with a group of soldiers to protect my lands and manor. I know both of you are in a safe pair of hands.'

'It is good of you to think this way. I can assure you that George and I only cared about Gytha's well-being. Not knowing you led us to be deceitful. It was not to be disloyal and for that I am sorry, my lord.'

'Let's not say any more about that, Godfrey. Let's just concentrate on making my lady happy, and I for one will make it my life's work.'

'Very well, my lord, what would you propose?'

'Why, that we make haste before I leave to serve William to make my dream come true and to make my lady safe from unwelcome advances until I return.'

'Then we must make haste and form a plan to suit all, my lord, if we are to have yourself and the Lady Gytha wed before you leave for the north.'

'We need to have speech, all three of us; however, you may inform the lady of my plans to return her to the title of Lady Gytha Bayeux, not Rowlands. She will then be safe and respected as my wife. I will hate the thought of leaving her but leave I'm afraid I will have to. I feel I will try hard to finish the battle quickly to ensure my speedy return.'

'I'm sure you will be back before we know it, Gilbert, absence makes the heart grow fonder.'

'We'll see, my old friend. I will leave it to you and hope that we can come to a mutual ending to our plight.'

'Peace then can resume at Alder-Sea manor once more and Normans and Saxons live together to make England prosper. I will speak for you, my lord, and press a little safety matter concerning myself, my lord,' Godfrey bowed his head, thinking it was of course the best solution. Gytha would be safe if she became Gilbert's wife. Yes, she would be safe from any Norman soldier. They would not dare to attack a Norman knight's manor, and if his old friend George was watching over her, he would be happy. Gytha was, after all, marriageable age already. His dear wife Marion had only been sixteen when he had married her, and they had been very happy and borne two children. Marion had mourned their daughter who died quite early on. Now, Godfrey was glad that she had not been alive to see their young son die at the side of Harold.

It was time to put the old differences to one side and become one nation. He was now sure the time for plotting was over. Why should anyone grieve more than they needed to? Godfrey was certain that Gytha would be cared for by Gilbert and not misused.

Chapter 10

Gytha looked into Godfrey's eyes. 'Marriage, my lord?' she said in hushed tones.

'Yes, my lady, he will not punish either of us, and William gave him leave to marry any of the maidens that he would have as wards to ensure his line flourished in England.'

'Marriage to a Norman, Godfrey. I fear Grandfather wouldn't have been happy about that,' she said, her fingers flying to her mouth.

'I understand, Gytha, but all Normans aren't cruel and uncaring. He would place you back as the lady of the household. Besides, I think that if your grandfather was alive, he would be happy to see you safe and cared for.'

'Godfrey, that was just what Grandfather wanted, to keep me safe.'

'I know, my lady, if he had known and been sure, he would have most certainly would have been most happy to give your hand in marriage to Gilbert, and instead of punishing me, he would make me your champion and protector.'

'He said that, Godfrey?'

'Yes, he will also leave my Lord Gunter to protect the manor with a number of soldiers to ensure our safety, so it makes sense to pay good intention to Gilbert's offer.'

'But marriage,' she whispered as her heart beat like a trapped bird as all manner of emotions tripped through her head.

'Your grandfather would have given you in marriage at some point, Gytha. You would not have been able to choose. So, at some point in your life, you would have to answer to a man as you did your grandfather and father before him.'

Gytha said, 'He does appear to be kind and understanding. I know naught of a married lady's life, Godfrey.'

'Believe me, my lady, he is kind and understanding. He thinks over matters carefully. He could have been harsher on both of us and chose not to.'

'Does he give us time for thinking about the offer, my lord? We need to understand and digest what my Lord Gilbert is asking of me.'

'We have little time, my lady. He wishes to wed you before he rides north to be at the side of William to help quell the uprising that is reported to be happening there.'

'So, I would at least have tonight to think and give him my answer on the 'morrow, my lord.'

'Me-thinks that would be possible, my lady. I understand his hurry. You need to give your vow of betrothal in our Good Father's presence, and it would be a least two weeks before your wedding, just enough time before he rides north.'

'Is the haste not unseemly, Godfrey?'

'No, my lady, I think you need to move quickly before he goes. We then have his cloak of protection.'

'Very well, Godfrey, if I must. To protect us, I will; however, I will have demands myself, one thing being although I will agree to marry him, he must leave me a maid in body until he returns. I will then become the wife when I have time to get used to the idea of lying with him. If he cares enough, I will be his wife in name, and sleep with him on his return.' This way she could be sure of why she liked him so.

'I'm sure, my lady, he would not agree to that. He will expect to be your husband when he marries you, no man will wait once married.'

'We'll see, my Lord Godfrey. We are to sup with him tonight. We will have speech tomorrow,' Gytha said with a pleasant smile that she did not feel inside. Her heart belied her words.

She needed speech with Enid who had gone to take their washing to the wash house. Enid would know how to approach this problem. Gytha knew inside that she liked Gilbert a lot but had no knowledge of being a wife. She had been quite young when her mother died, and the wonders of life had escaped her. Hopefully, Enid would find out what was expected of her. After all, she could not let him have all his own way, this would give her time to find out a wife's duties.

Godfrey smiled to himself. He understood what she was thinking, but as a man, he could not help her. As she said she must have speech with Enid, he would wait until she returned and then retire to his own solar until suppertime.

Enid returned to the solar to find Godfrey and Gytha sitting quietly by the fire. Both were deep in thought. Godfrey hoping that wherever George was, he would forgive him for not executing the plan he had for Gytha.

Gytha was thinking of how her Lord Gilbert would feel about waiting to consummate their marriage, and why she felt excited at the thought of marrying him. He excited her and intimidated her at the same time. His presence itself gave out overpowering strength and power. What would her grandfather feel about his kin marrying a Norman? Had he not wanted her to be as far away from them as she could? Yes, she did like him in a funny sort of way. She had from the first time she saw him, the searching look he had given her. Just as if he knew that she was a maid.

'My lady, I will take my leave and will join yourself and Gilbert at suppertime. We can then enjoy a pleasant supper with our lord.'

'Yes, Godfrey, my Lord Gilbert will call to escort me to supper. I hasten to say I will feel more comfortable with you dining with us.' Godfrey bowed his head and took his leave.

Gytha was also aware that he seemed somewhat relieved with the outcome of their speech with Gilbert. It appeared that neither of them were to be punished. And she agreed that he was too old to worry about her. He needed peace in his old age. And she would do what was needed to bring this about. Godfrey had served her grandfather with great loyalty to the end, and now she must fend for herself even though she was not schooled in womanly wiles.

Hopefully, Enid would be able to advise her. She had more to do with the married ladies in the village than Gytha, so she would have learnt things to pass on, and Gytha knew if she could be of a help to her, she would.

'Enid, I need to have speech with you. What do you know of wifely duties?'

'Wifely duties, Gytha, why would you be asking that?'

'I think I'm to marry my Lord Gilbert, and I know naught about wifely duties at all. It's a mystery to me. I would need to know how to conduct myself,' Gytha said going red.

'Why, Gytha, any man would be proud to take you to wife.'

'Yes, but what would be expected of me, Enid? I have no mother or married sister to advise me.'

'Well, I've never been married myself either, but I hear that when you lie with your husband that he will make love to you, and you will feel that you and he are the only two people in the world, you a maid and he a man. He will school you in the art of love, and some say its most enjoyable.'

'Yes, but how will I know what to do?'

'You would need to leave it to my Lord Gilbert, Gytha. He will guide you, and you have admitted that you like him, have you not?'

'Yes, he is so like the knights we dreamed of when we were children, so yes I do like him, and he makes my heart beat fast when he is near. He's so tall and strong.'

'I'm sure he will be kind as well as considerate. He has always struck me as a person who will think about things, and he is kind. Look how he visited every day when yourself and Godfrey were unable to look after yourselves. He made sure that you had the best care possible.'

'He did,' Gytha whispered.

'When did he tell you that he wished to be married to you?'

'Gilbert told Godfrey. He pointed out that I had not yet laid down my arms, and if I wanted to be re-instated as Lady Gytha of Alder-sea, I would have to marry him and be Lady Gytha Bayeux of Alder-sea. That way we would both get what we wanted, as King William gave him leave to choose from any maidens that became his wards.'

'The king has?' Enid whispered.

'Yes, and I became his ward as I am named Rowlands.'

'Has he not punished you in any way for deceiving him?'

'No, however, if I marry him willingly, he will leave Godfrey as my protector and Gunter to run the manor along with some soldiers for protection whilst he is away fighting in the north with William.'

'Perhaps he is kind as we have both said. You do like him, Gytha, don't you?'

'Aye, Enid, I do. Mind you, I wonder what Grandfather would think of it. He was so certain that he needed to get me to safety and yet my Lord Gilbert has proved him wrong.'

'Have you said yes you will marry him?'

'No not yet. I know I will, but I was going to ask him if we could be married and if he would wait until he came back from the north before I lay with him.'

'You can't do that, Gytha. Your marriage night has to be special, and I'm sure you will learn to respect and care for him. After all, he appears to be bothered about how you feel.'

'You think so, Enid?'

'I know so, my lady. I envy you. He's as handsome as any knight could be, and brave and strong. I wish it was me,' Enid said with a sigh.

For quite a while both maids became silent, and the two had the same thoughts. Enid, when would she have her knight in shining armour? She already admired her Lord Gunter, but she thought she was far beneath him, a lowly serf, and knowing this, she thought he would never turn his eyes to her. Gytha just sat and weaved dreams about Gilbert. Her thoughts were both exciting and fearful of becoming a married lady.

'You think I should lie with him as soon as we are married then?'

'Aye, I do. Then you can let it slip that I think Gunter is most handsome too, not that he would cast his eyes in my direction.'

'I have seen him watching you, Enid, and I'm sure it won't matter to a man that you are a serf if he likes you.'

'You think he likes me, my lady?'

'Yes, I do. You're not just any serf, Enid. You are now my lady-in-waiting and as such, you have elevated, and you really shouldn't keep going to the kitchens and helping them. Wally tends to take advantage of your good nature.'

'He perhaps is looking at me because my clothes are poor.'

'Aye, I will request that you have some new threads as you will be living in the castle and not in the kitchens. Perhaps then my Lord Gunter will be looking at you with new eyes. Enid, you are quite pretty in your own rights.'

'You think so, Gytha?'

'I do and if you become wed as well, we could perhaps compare notes,' both girls instantly broke out in laughter.

It was how Gilbert found them when he arrived to escort his Lady Gytha to supper. His breath caught in his throat as he set eyes on Gytha. She was now dressed in a sea green silk dress that seemed to cling to her slim body in all the places that mattered.

'Are you ready to take supper, sweet lady?' he said, his voice low and full of admiration.

'Yes, my lord,' Gytha answered, her cheeks blushing pink as she looked into his eyes.

'Make sure you have your supper brought to you, Enid, and when we have some gowns made for you, of course you will take supper in the hall. Gytha will need you with her for company when we men talk. It can sometimes be boring for the ladies,' and with a nod of his head, he took Gytha's hand in his. Gytha did not understand that by holding her hand he was claiming her for his own and making all aware that this maid belonged to him.

Sitting Gytha on his right next to Rolf, he sat Godfrey on his left. 'Are you fully rested, Godfrey?' he asked the old knight.

'I am, my lord.'

'Good,' he said turning his attention to Gytha and watching her make herself familiar with the soldiers and Saxons alike in conversation, jesting and making merry with ale. Everyone appeared to be at ease with one another. Who would have thought that a few sennights ago they were enemies? How quickly they had forged bonds of peace instead of war.

Yes, she could see that all Normans weren't the same. There was good and bad in Saxons as well as Normans, and peace would surely be good for all of them. Perhaps Grandfather was now looking down on her and was happy with the outcome of joining of Saxons and Normans if they could carve out a new and peaceful England in years to come.

Carving some meat from the huge wooden serving dishes, he placed a selection on the shared trencher and encouraged Gytha to eat a little, not once taking his eyes off her.

'Has Godfrey spoken to you, my lady?' he inquired.

'He has, my lord.'

'And what do you think of my solution?' he asked hopefully.

'I think it would be better if we had speech tomorrow, my lord, when we have time to think. My heart tonight belongs to my grandfather. I grieve for him, but you will have my answer tomorrow.'

'Your heart indeed would be held precious by any man, my lady,' he said in a soft voice.

Gytha's pulse raced as she felt a feeling that was alien to her. This man was making her warm all over. How could she bargain with him tomorrow? She was afraid that she would just fall into his arms. She needed to be able to have some bargaining tools left in her armoury to help her have a little of her own way, to keep a little in reserve, she thought. Still, tomorrow would soon come, and she needed to think tonight after supper to ensure she was in readiness for tomorrow.

Looking at him, she was not able to drag her gaze away from his face. She also realised that life would be interesting and exciting with this man. His eyes promised much. Enough for the thoughts in her head to make her feel hot all over.

Talk turned to joining William in the north, and Gilbert said, 'I hope it will be a swift, short battle so that we can return home to our life and families quickly,' he said looking at Gytha with meaning. The soldiers were beginning to get a little rowdy as they had supped more than enough of ale.

'Come, my lady, let me escort you safely back to your solar. Such talk is not meant for delicate maidens' ears,' standing and holding his hand out. They both walked out of the hall. He would return once Gytha was safely inside her solar.

Stopping at the door, he said, 'We must say our goodnights, sweet lady.' Still holding her hand with his, he gently caressed her. Suddenly gripping her face gently, he kissed her lightly on the lips. It was as if a butterfly had swiftly settled and then it had gone leaving her wondering and wanting more.

'Goodnight, sweet lady,' he whispered, waiting for her to turn and enter the solar before he marched down the corridor.

'Why, whatever is the matter, Gytha? You look as if you have been running, your cheeks are so pink.'

Gytha had her fingers to her lips as she whispered, 'He kissed me and called me his sweet lady. Oh Enid, I'm not sure that I could resist him. He is so much like the knight of my dreams. He has made a conquest, and I'm not sure that I should let him see my weakness for him.'

'Why not, my lady? You are obviously happy with his advances.'

'I know, Enid, but I'm afraid it might be the undoing of me. I need to keep a little mystery in my life, or I might bore him.'

'No, never, my lady. If you satisfy him, he will always be attentive and kind.'

'Are you sure, Enid? I'm not experienced in the art of womanly wiles.'

'I'm sure, my lady. He must want you, or he wouldn't want to marry you, now would he?'

'Perhaps marriage is the only way he thinks he will have me. There has been many a man that has married a good woman and taken harlots behind their back as fancy takes a man. I'm not sure I would be happy with that. It would be worse than a man that beat you and then what of love?'

'Love, my lady, you will know if you love him, and I'm sure my Lord Gilbert looks at you as if he does. He watches your every move. You may not think you love him, but methinks that he loves you.'

'You do?'

Enid looked at Gytha. 'Surely, my lady, that is not worthy of you. My Lord Gilbert is no liar. He appears to be caring and thinks deeply about all that matters. Give him the benefit of the doubt.'

'Do you think he will prove me wrong, Enid? You must have more faith in him than my grandfather.'

'Aye, Gytha, I have. I like him too, and I know inside you more than like him. Did he not watch you intently as Guy?'

'I'm sure there was something. I sometimes felt he could see right through my deceit.'

'And yet he never challenged you, my lady. I feel his feelings have always been there from the beginning, and he didn't quite understand why.'

'What would you do, Enid?'

'Why, I would marry him, my lady, and be glad that he was in my bed to protect me, for under his protection, no one would ever dare to hurt you. His love would always protect you, Gytha.'

'Then I must trust him with my heart as well as my body, Enid, for as a young girl I imagined a man that would never hurt me and always be there for me. So, you see, I will except nought else.'

'Gytha, even a Norman is capable of true feelings. You must see that. I fear your grandfather would have regretted sending you to a priory if he had time to know him better, and I also feel he would now approve of the match.' Enid looked at her old friend. She was indeed beautiful with her large lavender blue eyes framed with golden lashes, her blond curls and slim figure. Who wouldn't love her? As children, looks had never bothered them. They had always been surrounded by love and companionship. They needed nought else. Enid herself had felt like one of the family, and Lord George had always treated her well.

'Thank you, Enid, you make sense. Aye, I will agree to marry him, but I will still make sure I have some requests of my own. I can't let him have all his own way,' she said and both girls broke into laughter.

'Come, my lady, it's time to get ready to retire. We have a little wine. I will warm it by the fire while you wash, and don't forget that I have a fancy for Gunter,' she grinned as Gytha went to the bowl of water that she had just poured into the bowl. Once washed, they both sat in their shifts before a roaring fire.

'I declare I feel quite tired now. Enid, is your pallet comfortable enough?'

'It is, Gytha, much more comfortable than the outside shelter I shared. Goodnight, Gytha.' Enid lay down on her pallet and her mind turned to Gunter. He was a fine-looking knight, but he would not bother with the likes of a serving wench, even if she had been elevated to wait on Gytha. It certainly was not disagreeable. Gytha would always be her friend.

Enid slept soundly, whilst Gytha lay awake thinking of Gilbert and how tomorrow's speech with him would impact her life. She really did like him and felt that he would find her lacking as she knew naught of how a wife should act. How she wished her mother was still alive. She would have been able to counsel her on wifely duties. She would have also liked to know her mother. Lord Richard, her father, had told her that she was perfect, a miniature replica of her mother to remind him of how much he loved her. With God's grace, her father would perhaps be with his wife, Elise, reunited in death. How Gytha wished she was here now. Her mother was a married lady and could enlighten her with all the secrets of love. After all, she had not known her father to take another maiden after her mother died. If he had, Gytha had never known about it.

It was well into the night before Gytha eventually fell into a restless sleep. Her dreams were of Gilbert holding her tight whispering strange words to her that she could not understand. He was obviously speaking in his Norman tongue, and it frustrated her. Try as she might, she could not interpret the words and lay wide awake feeling cheated and that she needed to know what he was saying to her as he carried her towards a huge bed.

As Gytha lay there in the aftermath of her dream, she felt a warm feeling in her stomach and wanted to return to the dream to find out more of what happened when you lay with your husband. Sitting up, Enid already had hot water for her wash.

'Good morrow, Gytha, did you sleep well?'

'Yes, but methinks I had a lot on my mind. I will be feeling better after I have had speech with my Lord Gilbert and I know how he will react.'

'Tush. I'm sure it will go well, Gytha. You need not worry. He'll take one look at you and will give you everything you desire. Who could say no?'

Gytha appeared to think and answered, 'Well, if I recall, Grandfather loved me above all else, and he was able to say no to me on many occasions, as well as saying no to you.'

'I know, like the times we went to the woods, and he sent Godfrey to look for us, and he found that we had disobeyed him and played in the caves farther on than the dell. It was for a full sennight he wouldn't allow us to continue playing together.'

'I remember that clearly, Enid.'

'I know. I didn't dare come to speak to you. I would send Wulf and your grandfather would even send him packing with a flea in his ear,' Enid laughed.

'Well, I'll just have to think how I can get him not to say no to me. After all, he will love me like Grandfather but in a different way. It gets more annoying by the minute; most ladies would know immediately what to do.'

'Stop fretting, Gytha, you will soon learn how to use your looks and body; after all, men will give anything to have their way.'

'Aye, whatever it is they want. I don't know.'

'I swear you will soon learn, my lady. Make it up as you go along. Make sure you pamper yourself and look your best. I'm sure it will help. Now eat, my lady. Then you can get ready to make our Lord Gilbert willing to give you anything as well as his heart.'

Gytha walked over to the fresh bowl of water to have a wash, then stood looking at the bread and meat that had been sent from the kitchen to break her fast. She felt as if she would not be able to swallow anything because her stomach felt funny. She couldn't quite explain how she felt, it was in between excitement and fear. Perhaps it would be prudent just to quench her thirst.

'Do try to eat something, my lady. You will feel more like facing the interview ahead, and when you have, I'll have you looking like the most beautiful lady in all England, and he will give you anything for your favours.'

'That's just it, Enid, for my favours, and that's what I don't know about.'

'If you let my Lord Gilbert take the lead, you don't need to know. He will be very happy to show you, and all you will have to do is convince him that he has made you happy.'

'He might be disappointed at my lack of experience and then won't give even a little of his power over.'

'Well, it's for certain that he would not be happy if you had experience of some other lord. He would not then be interested in wedding you, so be satisfied and let him lead you. Trust me, it will work.'

Once Enid had helped Gytha to dress in her lavender blue dress that matched her eyes, she sat brushing her curls until they shone. She urged Gytha to apply a little rose water to her body that they had made themselves with herbs and dried rose petals. The warmth of the body sent out a slight smell of fresh roses that was not too overpowering that most men would appreciate.

Now they could do no more, so sitting down, they patiently waited for her lord to request her presence. The request came in the form of Godfrey.

'It is time, my lady, for us to attend to matters with our Lord Gilbert. I hope it won't take long and will be satisfactory to both of you.'

'I too, Godfrey; however, I can't help being a little affeered and still wonder what my grandfather would think.'

'Don't worry, my lady, I'm sure Gilbert will deal gently with you. He is not the ogre we thought. He is quite gentle and understanding. I swear he always thinks matters through before making any decisions, and as for Lord George, I'm sure he will be pleased with the outcome.'

Gytha noticed that Godfrey was today smartly dressed and wondered what the occasion was. She didn't have a mind to ask him as her thoughts were too mixed with the speech she was to have with Gilbert.

'You will need your cloak, my lady, it's a chilly morning.'

Gytha looked at Godfrey in an enquiring way, 'Surely we are to have speech in the disputes room, and it won't be chilly in there.'

'We are to put Lord George to rest first, my lady, had you forgot?' Gytha gasped and put her hand to her mouth. Surely she was wicked. She had quite forgot about her grandfather lying in the chapel.

'Oh, my Lord Godfrey, how selfish I've been the last few days. I've been wrapped up in my own problems and wondering what Grandfather would think. I had quite forgotten that he needed to be put at rest.'

'Well, I dare say, he would forgive you as he will be aware of what troubles you and that can quickly be amended after. He requests that Enid would like to join us.'

'Of course, Godfrey. Take one of my cloaks, Enid. There is one in an autumn brown and a dress to match. It won't take you long to pop it on, and we'll be ready to go,' she said, smiling at Godfrey.

She moved over to the rail that held her cape while she took the matching blue cloak with the hood trimmed with fur, placing it ready to put on. Gytha went into her chest of clothes and took out a small clasp that denoted her family crest to show that she was a Rowlands. Her father had the goldsmith to make it fashioned as her late mother's. Gytha very rarely wore it. Today was special, and she wanted the Normans present to know she was of noble birth. Enid appeared from behind the rough wooden screen wearing the brown dress. It really suited her. She helped Gytha on with her cloak, and Godfrey gallantly held the brown one for Enid to put on.

'You look very fair, Enid. The colour suits you, very becoming,' he added.

Chapter 11

With Gytha being led by Godfrey, Enid walked demurely at the other side. Gilbert was waiting for them in the main room. He only seemed to look at Gytha, offering his hand to her without speaking.

Soon the little procession made their way to the chapel where the small fat priest, Father Bernard, was waiting, looking very nervous. He was unsure of Gilbert yet and having not met him before, he certainly was not altogether aware of his ways. He had also heard of manors that had been sacked and burnt and the village priests had been run through by the Norman soldiers who had no regards for human life. One could almost see him trembling as he stood at the altar.

There was just a handful of people that attended the burial. Father Bernard quietly gave George the holy rites of burial and walked in front of the coffin to the small churchyard that housed the graves of his wife and two sons. They at last would all be reunited in death.

Gytha felt at peace and a little closer to her family because she would be taken care of by her Lord Gilbert. She would be able to walk to their graves and reflect whenever she wished. Gytha could not help but think they would watch over her and protect her as well. Her answer had come to her as she stood there. She would become Gilbert's wife, and hopefully she would be a dutiful wife and Gilbert himself would school her into what to do.

She would be truthful and explain that she had no idea what a wife's duties were in the bedroom. She had only been trained in housewifely duties and recently in a serf's duties. She smiled ruefully at the thought. Gytha would be more understanding now because she knew how it felt to be a servant even though her time as a serf was short.

Standing and watching the churls cover her grandfather's grave with soil, she was unable to stop the stray tear from sliding down her cheek and was surprised as Gilbert gently pressed a posy of early spring flowers into her hand to place on George's grave. Blue eyes met grey and Gytha realised that there would be a greater understanding between this maid and the Norman knight. It just required a little more understanding on her part. Hadn't Gilbert up until now been more than caring? He could have punished both Godfrey and her, and he had chosen not to. Gilbert had only been kind and helpful, and now it was her turn to look at how she acted.

As Father Bernard made to take his leave, Gilbert said, 'Come back with us, Father, and partake a goblet of wine. I may have a further task for you to oversee.'

'Of course, my Lord Gilbert,' the timid priest answered wondering what he would want of him. He had no outstanding duties to attend to. It would be Thursday before he needed to attend the hearings and complaints with his master and that was at least five days away. So, he was unsure of what they required of him unless it was the prisoners that had shot Godfrey and Gytha down in the woods. The small group of people made their separate ways to home, leaving Gytha and the two knights and Father Bernard to return to the main hall.

'Godfrey, can I leave Father Bernard in your safe hands whilst I have speech with my lady? Then I will advise you of the outcome. Enjoy some refreshment as this could take some time. If you wish for anything to eat, Godfrey will send Wulf to the kitchens for you.' Holding his hand out for Gytha's, he led her to the disputes room, quietly shutting the huge oak door behind him.

'Well, my lady, have you thought more of what Godfrey and I spoke of yesterday?'

Gytha blushed, and her cheeks turned a delicate pink. 'I have, my lord, and I am unsure of what being wed means. That is,' she rushed her words, 'I am aware of housewifely duties, but I'm afraid I know naught of wifely duties. Perhaps it would be better if I learnt more before I agreed to wed you, my lord.'

Gilbert threw his head back and laughed, 'My lady, no man would want their intended to learn the secrets of the bedchamber before marrying. It is something a husband and wife school themselves together.' Gytha looked up at him blue eyes wide open and trusting. Her Lord Gilbert was more amenable than she hoped for.

'Perhaps, my lord, we could think more about it whilst you are away with William?'

'No, my lady, I need for your sake as well as mine to see you safely wed and looked up to as my wife before I leave to serve at William's side.'

'Why, my lord, am I in danger?'

'No, sweet lady, it just means that you will be respected as the head of this household until I return. I don't want to drag you to the altar. I would prefer you to agree; however, we will be wed, my lady. I could persuade you by other methods, my lady,' he said taking a step towards her. Gytha immediately stepped backwards and would have fallen. Gilbert was too quick, catching hold of her before she fell. He pulled her to his body in a strong embrace. Her breath catching in her throat, she looked up at him. It was not fear of being hurt, it was fear of being close to him and not being able to resist him that unnerved her.

He surprised her by saying, 'We must not go to the altar without knowing each other a little, my sweet lady,' as he began to feather soft kisses on her forehead and down to her eyes, gently making his way to her mouth. Gilbert felt her body tremble as his mouth roamed further down her neck and throat.

'There, my sweet lady, don't tell me you don't want to experience a little more,' he breathed as he held her gaze and caressed her waist.

Gytha licked her lips as he held her tightly. ''Twas quite nice,' she breathed without thinking.

''Twill be nicer still on our wedding day. So, will you come to me as a wife willingly?' he asked as he continued to woo her with his hand tracing the contours of her face.

'I fear, my lord, I have no experience of wifely duties.'

'Let me worry about that, sweet lady. I will surely enjoy instructing you, and I would never hurt you, I promise.'

'You wouldn't and you promise,' was the only reply she gave.

'I do. So, what will it be? Do I have to drag you to the altar or will you come willingly to my side? I promise I will always look after Godfrey as well.'

'Aye, my lord, I will if it will bring peace to Alder-Sea. I hope my grandfather, wherever he may be, will be pleased for me,' she said quietly.

'Aye, I'm sure he will be, my lady. Now we must give Godfrey and Enid the good news and take our betrothal vows. You do like me a little, my lady?' he enquired as he once more stroked her face.

'Aye, my lord, a little,' she smiled back at him nervously. Gilbert could not help but take her lips in a much stronger kiss, the longing for her more urgent than he thought. He needed to compose himself before he joined Father Bernard.

Father Bernard stood as Gilbert and Gytha strode into the room.

'Good news, Godfrey, your Lady Gytha has done me the honour of agreeing to become my wife.'

'She has, my lord?' Godfrey sighed in relief.

'The Lady Gytha has, and it would please us so if you would hear our betrothal vows, Father Bernard.'

'Of course, my lord,' came the nervous answer.

Gytha and Gilbert solemnly said their vows. Godfrey spoke up at this point. 'Perhaps Gunter and I can ride to the market in the next village and bring whatever my Lord Gilbert and my lady need for the wedding.'

'Are you feeling strong enough, Godfrey? You had quite a spill and haven't been on your feet long,' Gytha said, not wanting the old knight to leave her. She was suddenly aware of what she had promised to do and would feel safer with him around.

'I do, my lady.'

'Perhaps my Lady Gytha is right. You need to rest longer. There will be other tasks for you to complete,' Gilbert stepped in to ensure that they protected the old knight.

'Perhaps you are right, my lord,' Godfrey conceded. Giving Gytha a searching look, it was as if he had looked into her heart and mind to see the nervousness that had suddenly swamped her being.

'I will ride myself and choose new threads for my lady with Gunter. We will bring something pretty for Enid to wear as well, my lady, as she will attend you, as there are no other ladies that you are close to.'

'There is no rush, my Lord Gilbert, we have plenty of time. We have only just promised to each other.'

'I'm afraid we must wed within the two weeks, my lady, as I will be joining my Lord William in the north, and I feel for your safety we need to leave you a married lady and not a maiden.'

'Is such haste seemly, my lord?'

'It is necessary, my sweet lady. I will feel at ease knowing that you have the protection as lady of the manor and will have Rolf and Godfrey to watch over you.' Gytha just looked at him hoping that the alarm she was feeling did not show on her face.

'You will, my lord,' she whispered.

'I will, my sweet lady,' he looked at her with smouldering grey eyes.

'I will away to my solar then and ready myself for supper with your permission,' she said her voice firmer and more controlled.

'Allow me to escort you safely to your solar, and then I will call to escort you to supper, my lady,' he smiled.

If Gytha thought that she would have her own way, she realised that she would have to be more inventive, for my Lord Gilbert had made up his mind that he would be in charge.

Still, she would have time to invent a few twists whilst he was away to the north, but then her heart went in another way. Did she really want him to leave? Try as she might, the answer was no, she would feel safer if he remained here, even if she had to come to terms with the wifely duties. Looking down at his hand holding hers, she felt safe with him. Grandfather had taught her to be afraid of the Normans, but try as she might, she could not be afraid of this one. He was tall, strong and yet gentle. What more would you like a knight to be when he swept you off your feet? *There is nothing more that you could want,* she counselled herself. Gilbert had everything that a maiden would wish for, everything that she could possibly want. Her mind whispered, *I'm sorry, Grandfather,* without a sound being uttered.

Stopping at the door, he gently lifted her hand to his lips and kissed it. 'I will be back, sweet lady,' he uttered, and then he was gone.

Gytha stood and watched as he strode away without looking back, trying to steady her treacherous heart. It would only do as it wanted, and Gytha had no control over it. She had feelings for this Norman, and there was no way that she could change it.

Gytha realised that she would fall in with his plans, and each time that she thought that she wouldn't, he would change her mind with a look or a caress. Gytha walked and sat on the steps leading to the bailey. She felt that she needed a little time to herself before going in to Enid.

Sitting there, she could only think of Gilbert and that in a couple of weeks she would be his wife and that meant that she would be answerable to him and him alone. There would be no more wandering and rides on her own, no more acting as a young maiden. She would be a married lady and have to cover her hair with a coif.

I best go in to Enid and ready myself for supper, else I won't be ready when he comes for me, and that wouldn't do. She needed more than ever to follow instructions. There was many a time when she was younger that they had strayed against Grandfather's wishes, but it would not be taken as a married lady if she did not.

Walking back to her solar, she found Enid waiting for her return. 'Where have you been, Gytha? I heard my Lord Gilbert escort you back and him walk away, but you did too but only after his steps vanished.'

'I needed time alone, Enid, to think, but I'm afraid I didn't arrive at any answers.'

'You did not give your lord his answer then.'

'Yes, I did, Enid. We are to be wed in two weeks, and it seems so quick, and not quite seemly.'

'Are you afraid, my little friend? I would be as well,' Enid said with great sympathy.

'Aye, a little, Enid.'

'It's natural, Gytha. We will all be when it's our time to wed, you'll see. I'm sure your Lord Gilbert will be gentle and kind. It seems not to harm any of the married ladies in the village.'

'I suppose not,' Gytha said begrudgingly.

'Well, we best get you ready for supper, my lady, or else your lord will be here and have to wait.' Gytha smiled and began to take her clothes off to freshen up.

Soon she was ready and sitting in the chair waiting for Gilbert, and it wasn't a moment too soon, as the scratching came at the door and when Enid opened it, Gilbert was there smiling.

'Is your mistress ready?'

'Yes, my lord.'

'Good and I see you still have on the pretty dress that Gytha told you to put on, so you will sup in the main hall tonight with myself and your mistress. Gunter is here to escort you.'

Enid blushed as she observed Gunter behind her lord.

'Would you wait a second, my lord? Enid needs some rose water.'

'Of course, sweet lady,' he said.

Enid quickly washed her face behind the screen and splashed on rose water, and they were ready, Gytha hand in hand with Gilbert and Gunter surprisingly holding Enid's hand.

The Norman soldiers and Saxons were jesting with each other as they entered the hall for supper. Gilbert placed Gytha on his right, and next to him sat Gunter with Enid, and Rolf was at the other side. Once more, Gilbert made sure that Gytha had meat on her side of the shared trencher. Using one hand to eat, he grasped her hand under the table. He needed to touch her. He wished that they were wed already and could retire to the solar together. He would be patient. He would be travelling to the market armed with Gytha's measurements for a dress for her wedding day, and he would purchase two gowns for Enid. Enid had done well taking care of Gytha and that pleased him.

Tomorrow, he would take Gytha riding. He realised that Star was her horse and hoped that she was a good rider. He wanted to see her at ease in his company, and what better way to achieve that other than out riding together.

Chapter 12

He came promptly after he had broken his fast, 'Good morning, sweet lady, I have your horse saddled and ready to ride. Star is yours, is she not?'

Gytha smiled, showing a dimple in her cheek, 'Yes, my lord, you have guessed correctly.'

'I think I knew the day your grandfather rode out with me. The mare surely recognised you and appeared to love you as I do,' he whispered close to her ear.

'I would have loved to have accompanied you and Grandfather on that ride, my lord.'

'Methinks we will have many such enjoyable times to come in the future, sweet lady,' as he took hold of her hand.

'We will,' was the only thing she could think of to say. At times like this, he made her heart beat like a trapped bird in her chest. Yes, she was afraid of what would happen in the bedchamber, but at times like this it seemed trivial. He was kind, considerate and caring, was there naught to be frightened of?

''Twill not take me long, my lord,' she smiled at him in a beguiling way.

'Then I will leave for a little while longer, sweet lady. I will return in a short while.'

Once Gilbert had left, promising to return, Gytha made haste in breaking her fast and as soon as she finished, quickly made ready to go riding.

'Methinks you are going to enjoy your dalliance with my lord,' Enid said with a laugh.

'Tush, Enid, I'm just looking forward to riding Star. In case you hadn't noticed, I've had little time for such enjoyable pastimes for a while,' Gytha said with a smile.

'It is good then that Lord Gilbert is to accompany you on your ride to ensure you do not venture too far in the forest, my lady. It is said there are rebel soldiers abroad.'

'Who said this?' Gytha asked inquiringly.

'Why, it's common knowledge, my lady, that Gilbert and his followers have rounded up another two soldiers that attacked you and Godfrey and are now languishing in the guardhouse. Gilbert has held a trial and they are to be hung for their evil deeds. As long as they were free in the forest, they would be able to attack others, and our lord wishes that everyone can ride without being hurt or accosted.' Gytha looked thoughtful as she dwelled on the information. Gilbert was right, visitors as well as villagers needed to be safe whilst riding abroad.

Gilbert returned to find Gytha ready and waiting, 'Are you ready for our ride, my lady?'

Smiling back, Gytha assured him that she was eager to be reunited with her beloved Star and would enjoy riding with him. 'I have missed these simple pleasures, my lord.'

Walking into the stables, Star immediately whinnied at the sight of Gytha who at once stroked his velvet muzzle whispering how much she had missed and loved him. Gilbert gently pulled her away and into his arms.

'Have you a few sweet words for me, my lady? As I said before, we need to discover a little more about each other before we wed, my sweet,' he said as he held her tightly in his embrace letting his lips slip down towards her cleavage making her tremble in his arms. Gytha was not schooled in the art of love and as Gilbert came up for air, it was obvious what he was thinking. Gytha grasped at anything to stop the thundering in her ears.

'Tell me, my lord, what is your horse's name?' Gilbert smiled ruefully as the innocent question had quickly cooled his ardour. Irritable at the thought, he could have quite easily taken her there and then. He wanted her so much. He realised in time this lady was to be his wife, and he only had two weeks to wait before he could lay with her.

'Come, my lady, or we might dally here too long.' He helped her upon her gentle Star, mounted his horse, and said, 'He is named Lightning. He is as fast as the shock of lightning in the sky and would quite easily carry both of us to safety if need be.'

'You must trust him a lot, my lord.'

'Yes, I do. He has helped me in battle more than I can remember, strong and fleet of foot, my lady.'

'I'm pleased to know that, my lord. He will carry you safely back to Alder-sea after the battle in the north,' she said shyly.

'You will be pleased to see me return then, my lady, when I arrive back?'

'I think all will rejoice at your return. The villagers are now accepting you in my grandfather's place and look to you for guidance.'

'You think so?'

'I have walked among the villagers and heard them talk. They have taken to you, my lord.'

'And you, sweet lady, not the villagers. How will you feel?

'You will by then be my husband. I'm sure every lady is happy to see their spouse return.'

Gilbert went quiet. Gytha had sidestepped the question. He wanted a declaration of sorts, and all she had done was blush and look downwards. Hopefully, he could change her mind in the bedchamber. Being a lover was not new to him. He lived by the sword and could die by the sword, so, he had taken advantage of a different paradise before he went to the eternal one.

He knew once he had Gytha he would not be satisfied with anyone else. He was in love and naught else would do. Slowing his horse to a stop, he slipped from Lightning's back. Holding his arms up to her, he helped her from Star's back.

Looking down at her, he asked again, 'And you, my fair maiden, will you be pleased to see me back? Yes or no and for what reason?' Looking down into her blue eyes he waited for the answer he wanted.

Gytha looked up at him feeling very small, unable to drag her eyes away from his, 'Because I would miss you, my lord, as I knew I would when I was Guy and Grandfather was sending me away. I felt safe with you around.'

Pulling her to him, he rained small kisses on her face. Then he took her mouth. 'How do you feel now, here in my arms, Gytha? Safe, do you like the feeling of being close?'

'Aye, my lord.'

Lightning and Star were quietly lipping the grass. Gilbert pulled her onto the grass beside him, for once not able to control his feelings. He was very near to being carried away. His hand had begun to caress her hips, and he could feel that Gytha was also giving into her feeling.

Jumping up and pulling her to her feet he said, 'We must wait, sweet lady. I know by your reaction to my ardour that you have feelings for me and that is all I need to make me patient for a little longer. Just two short weeks, my lady. Come, let's walk partway back, that way I can feel closer by holding your hand.'

Walking hand in hand and leading their mounts, they walked quietly back to the village, both mulling over their thoughts. Gytha felt wanton. She would have willingly let her Lord Gilbert lie with her in the grass, and she a lady. Gytha knew this was wrong before marriage and knew of maidens that had fallen foul of amorous men. Grandfather would have been angry. Aye, she had lay in his arms and was excited at his touch, but he had been considerate and thought of her. She had been aware that he had wanted to lie completely with her, and he had stopped himself. That was a good sign, wasn't it? she thought.

Gilbert felt much the same as he squeezed her hand. He was glad that he hadn't let his feelings have free reign. He wanted to take her to his bed a married woman. His mother would be shocked to know that he had lay with any maiden, let alone almost let his feelings take his betrothed before marriage.

'I am not sorry, sweet lady, for our interlude back then. I know more than ever that you care for me. I have watched you as Guy and couldn't help my feelings. Looking at your beauty is what smote my heart, and it will always belong to you now as I hope yours will be mine.' He waited for Gytha's answer.

'Aye, my lord, I will always hold you dear in my heart. I too felt strange as I lay in the grass. I'm sure you will instruct me in the art of the bedchamber. I just hope I won't disappoint you, my lord.'

'Never, sweet lady,' he said as he kissed her gently. Holding hands, they walked back through the castle gates. Some would say they looked very happy. The villagers thought they looked contented.

As one married lady said to her husband, Abe, 'Lady Gytha looks contented at last, my love.'

'So do Lord Gilbert, my love. I vow he'll be more than contented in a couple of weeks,' he smiled back at his wife. Both of them went back to their work. Life at Alder-Sea was settling down contentedly. The fear of the war was over, and most people had accepted the Normans as their new lords. And Gilbert Bayeux appeared to be fair and understanding overlord.

Chapter 13

Preparation for their lord and lady's wedding began. Godfrey and Rolf went hunting to make sure there was enough in the stores for the whole of the village to join in the feasting afterwards. Gunter and Gilbert rode to the market a few miles away to buy gowns for Gytha and Enid. He even allowed himself a new tunic and leggings. He made sure that Gytha had all the fripperies that she needed on such an important day. He also purchased a bride gift for Gytha, a gold ring and neck circlet in Welsh gold. He hoped she would be pleased with it.

When Godfrey and Gilbert carried the huge chest full of wedding clothes, she was amazed at how much he had purchased. As Gytha delved into the chest, she drew out a white muslin gown with small roses and seed pearls decorating the neck and hem with a matching cloak if the day was cool.

Gytha's cheeks flamed red as she drew out new silk shifts to wear. He had also thought of undergarments. For Enid, he had chosen pink muslin.

The roses in the gardens were just beginning to bloom. He would instruct the gardener of the manor on the day of the wedding to decorate the church with pink and white roses and to fashion his lady a band of pink and white roses for her head. He had sent word to his mother and father of his impending wedding. He knew it would be impossible for them to attend since they would be wed before they could make it to England. He knew his mother would be more than pleased. She had given up on him ever getting married. At least he would have been doing something right in her eyes.

There was an air of anticipation at Alder-Sea as Gytha's wedding day approached, and Gytha was getting more worried by the day. When she had lain in the grass with Gilbert, everything had seemed easy to Gytha. Gilbert had been in control of his feelings. He appeared to have stopped, leaving her feeling that she wanted more. What was more, though? she thought. What were the mysteries of the marriage bed? She was aware now that you would only find out if you were a married lady. It was in this state of mind that Enid found her.

'You look troubled, Gytha?'

'No more than usual, Enid. My mind still wonders about wifely duties. Lord Gilbert has kissed me and roused many feelings within me that I wasn't aware I had, but then drew back leaving me wanting more.'

'And so he should draw back. You must stay chaste until you take your wedding vows. You were raised properly, Gytha.'

'Enid, I felt as if I wanted more, was that wrong of me?'

'No, my friend, but it would have been wrong if you had gone farther. It is only nights away, and then you both can enjoy the delights of marriage.'

'You know, Enid, although I'm a little affeered, I am quite looking forward to my marriage night, although I'll not be a maiden any longer, just a married lady.'

'Believe me, my lady, if it was myself and Gunter, I would willingly become a married lady.' Both Gytha and Enid doubled up with laughter.

'If you ever do become a married lady, we must compare notes, Enid,' at this statement neither Gytha or Enid could control themselves, not even when Gilbert and Gunter came to collect them for supper. Both men were quite intrigued at what had started the two ladies on their bout of mirth that didn't seem to get any better as they approached the main hall.

Gilbert stopped and said, 'Gytha, try and control yourself. It's not seemly to laugh so loud. You can tell me what mishap has brought you to this state after supper. We will take a walk, now control yourself.' After Gilbert's gentle words, she dare not look at Enid; both felt a little chastised.

Neither Enid or Gytha dared to look at each other in case they burst out laughing again. One thing was certain to Gytha; she was sure that Gunter only had eyes for Enid. Gytha was sure it would be a love match. She then began to question if Gilbert really loved her or was he marrying her to cement Normans and Saxons through marriage?

After supper, Gunter stood and asked Enid if she would walk with him a little. For once at a loss for words, she smiled and agreed.

'You won't need me for a while, my lady?' she asked looking at Gilbert.

'Not for a while, Enid. Gytha and myself will walk in the gardens for a little before I return her to her solar. We still have a little drink to finish.' He was giving Gunter time to choose his route to walk in. He would then take a walk with Gytha. Even though he had held her close, he felt the need to hold her again. Tomorrow he would be wed to her and his needs satisfied.

The arrival of a young soldier yesterday had made him aware that he would have one night only with his bride before he rode to William's side to quell the uprising in the north. He was disappointed to be leaving her so soon, but he was loyal to his king as well. It would be hard for Enid and Gunter too. He was aware that his friend was in love with the gentle Enid and would talk of marriage on Gilbert's and Rolf's return from the north. God willing that they would return safely. He was certain that Godfrey and Gunter would watch over his Lady Gytha and Enid for him whilst he was away. It would be hard telling her that he must leave her after only one night of married life.

Standing and holding his hand out for hers, he led her into the gardens through a pathway of roses and onto the dovecotes where the work on building outside shelters had gone well. Two privies stood far away from the shelters at the back, and a number of completed roundhouses stood neatly in rows. Yes, there would be extra shelter for impending visitors now. The manor would not be ashamed of their guest accommodation which was certainly an improvement.

Drawing Gytha into the shadows of the building, he pulled her into his arms, holding her against his strong frame. He bent once more to take her lips, whispering words to her that she did not understand. Gytha was willing him to talk in her own tongue so that she could understand what he said. It frustrated her because he made her feel wanton. She wanted whatever it was there and then, and it was not seemly for her to feel this way. There was a promise of something, and she wanted whatever it was. Her stomach was aflutter, and she could not help pushing herself against him.

'I fear we must go back, my sweet lady. We need to wait until we wed; just a short while, my sweet. Both you and I will taste the delights of being wed. I promise you I will always be gentle, sweet maid.' Loosing his arms from around her, he took her hand and led her back to the manor, stopping only as a flushed Enid and Gunter joined them at the entrance.

'Did you enjoy your walk, Gilbert?' Gunter asked.

'Very much and you and Enid?'

'I need to have speech with you before you are wed, Gilbert.'

'Of course, we will escort these two maidens back to their solar and go back to the main hall. We can converse over a last goblet of wine, my friend.'

'Goodnight, sweet ladies,' Gilbert said, kissing Gytha's hand. 'I will join you tomorrow at the church, my lady.' Taking their leave, Gilbert and Gunter walked away leaving the two maidens as they entered the solar.

'Well, my friend, what is it you need to get out in the open?' Gilbert asked.

'I have asked Enid to become betrothed to me, and she has agreed to, with your blessing, of course.'

'I have seen it coming, my friend, and of course, you have my blessing, but you will have to show the same courtesy to William. You will have to converse with him, and I'm sure his answer will be yes too.'

'I wished I could have come to this conclusion before and perhaps I would have been able to get our wedding in before you left. I will have to wait until you return. I envy you, Gilbert.'

'I can say I can't wait until the morrow, Gunter. All my heart's desires will be mine, and I can say I won't want another maiden other than Gytha.'

'Gilbert, you need to retire. You need your strength for tomorrow. Perhaps after your wedding, our good Father Bernard will hear mine and Enid's betrothal vows before he leaves.'

'Perhaps I can take a message to William with your request, and we can see if his answer can return quickly to you, although I will be sorry I cannot be there on your day, Gunter.'

The two friends went to the passageway to make their way to their solars. Gunter made his way along the passageway to his own after bidding Gilbert goodnight. Gilbert stopped outside his solar. It was so near to the one occupied by Gytha. Just a wall separated them. Tomorrow, nought would separate them. He would have the strength to await tomorrow.

Entering his solar, he threw a log on the fire to bring a little more warmth to the chamber. Quickly divesting himself of his clothes, he jumped under the covers to await the morning. His clean set of clothing hung ready, and he had asked for a bath to be brought to his solar before he broke his fast to cleanse his body. He also knew that one would be taken to Gytha's solar to for her to bathe. Their wedding was to be at noon, and there would be merrymaking throughout the day with all joining in. Gilbert was tired but lay awake thinking of his bride. He eventually fell asleep in the early hours of the morning.

Gilbert lay in his bath soaking in the sweet- smelling water. His threads had been laid out for him by Wulf. He would break his fast before he dressed. Lying in the water, he could not help but feel excited at the prospect of lying with his new wife tonight or being disappointed that he would be leaving her tomorrow morning to follow William. However, follow him he must. This time tomorrow he would be taking his leave of Gytha, and she was not aware of it yet. Rising and climbing out of the water, he was soon dried and encased in a robe. Just in time, Wulf came back from the kitchens carrying his bread and meat along with a flagon of fresh ale.

Gytha had already been waited on by Enid, who made sure that she had bathed and applied rose water to her delicate skin. Her golden curls had been washed and shone like spun gold. Before Grandfather had cut her hair, it had been long, falling to her waist.

'It's a shame, Gytha, it will take many moons to grow your hair again.'

'It is far easier to wash this length, Enid, so I don't mind too much. Now send the serf that's standing outside for someone to empty the bath. You need fresh water as well.'

'I can manage with hot water and the bowl behind the screen, Gytha. You will look beautiful in the dress that Lord Gilbert has chosen for you.'

'If you're sure you can manage, Enid, then we can break our fast before they take away the bath, and dress afterwards.' Gytha wrapped herself in a warm woollen robe, the sleeves falling into a pointed shape at the back.

Enid took her hot water behind the screen and cleansed her body then washed her dark hair. Once Enid had rubbed her hair dry on some clean material, she combed it straight. Once it had dried, she would pin it up after she dressed. She was excited at the thought of Gunter seeing her in the pretty pink dress. She couldn't believe that she was now promised to him, and she too would become a married lady.

Enid waited for the kitchen maid who had taken her place to bring in the food for them to break their fast and asked for two serfs to remove Lady Gytha's bathtub. They would then be ready to dress Gytha's hair and have her ready to be escorted to the church.

The seamstress and another lady had been busy from early morning dressing the altar and the pews with garlands to match the rose garland for her lady's headdress. The two dresses were hanging side by side ready for Gytha and Enid; both felt special for different reasons. Gytha because she was to wed Lord Gilbert, and Enid because she would be dressed in fine threads thanks to Gilbert and Gunter.

It was nearing eleven when Enid said, 'If we are both to be ready for Godfrey to escort us to the church, we must make haste and begin to dress, my lady.'

'Oh, Enid, I feel quite nervous now. I don't know if my stomach is excited or nervous.'

'I think it's both, my lady. You just leave everything to Gilbert. I'm sure he will be most considerate. He will make you happy, and you him.'

'I hope so, Enid. To marry is a long time if you don't suit each other.'

'Don't fret, let's just make sure you look your best.'

Gytha stood, and Enid put more rose water on her body, slipped a fresh silk shift over her head, and placed over her head her new bride's gown of white muslin. She had to admit it fitted perfectly with the tiny artificial rosebuds sewn around the bustline and around the hem.

'Enid, it looks beautiful and fits perfectly.'

'You make the dress, Gytha. You are perfect. It's no wonder Lord Gilbert wants to wed you so quickly,' Enid said, giggling.

'You must put your dress on before doing my hair and then I'll do yours, Enid.' At that moment there came a scratch at the door. It was Rolf bringing the crown of pink and white roses for Gytha's headdress.

'I will see you both at the church my ladies.'

'Thank you, Rolf,' they both answered. Soon Enid had Gytha's hair brushed and dressed with the coronet of fresh roses. Gytha set to and dressed Enid's hair, taking one small rose and pinning it in her hair.

That's the one thing that Gytha wished, that Grandfather had not cut her hair. It was the fashion for ladies to wear their hair long. Still, Grandfather had acted as he had to protect her. She wished that he was still alive to attend her wedding. As it was, she had no living relative in attendance, although Godfrey was like a second father or grandfather to her. He only had her welfare at heart. It would soon be Gilbert who would be her protector, and she could only feel that she would be safe with him.

'Let me look at you, Enid. You look so becoming in that dress. Pink suits you, my friend. Gunter will want to marry you today, I'll be bound.' Gytha smiled at her old playmate passing her some more rose water to use.

'Gytha, I feel I dare not sit down in case I crease myself,' she giggled.

'I feel the same, my friend. We are young ladies now, not brawling children in the forest. It's not pretend anymore, it's for real,' she said in hushed tones.

Chapter 14

'You look beautiful, Gytha. The dress that your lord chose really suits your fair colouring.'

'You think so, Enid? I was just thinking that my Lord Gunter will want to wed you today. I have never seen you looking so fair.'

'Thank you, my friend,' Enid replied.

'This is where you belong, with me. It suits you far better than having Wally box your ears for spilling the drink or ruining a trencher,' Gytha said with a laugh.

Enid's hand stretched out for the copper plate. She could not believe the girl that looked back at her was herself. She had to admit that she could now be mistaken for a lady. A thought ran through her head. Gunter had asked her to be his wife so in a way she would be a lady. Her heart was lost. Even if Gunter had been a serf, she would have loved him. Her heart had been smote by his looks and smile since first she set eyes on him. It was fair to say Gunter made her heart sing, and she hoped that she would not have to wait long before she could lie with him beside her.

There was a loud scratching at the door, and Enid opened the door to Godfrey. 'You look very fair today, Enid. I didn't recognise you.'

'Thank you, Lord Godfrey,' Enid said demurely.

'I'm here to escort you to the church, my Lady Gytha. Your grandfather would have been so proud of you,' Godfrey said, his eyes watering slightly as he spoke of his old friend.

'I am pleased to have you at my side, Godfrey, who better when I can't have Grandfather?' she said, smiling at him to try and not cause more grief to the elderly knight. He had been part of her life for as long as she could remember.

The small party left the solar, Gytha leaning on Godfrey's arm, and Enid following behind. Villagers lined the pathway to the church. Whispers of how beautiful our lady was, some threw rose petals in front of her. Wulf was standing at the door of the church to open the door for Gytha to enter.

Standing at the altar, Gilbert watched his bride walk towards him. He was lost, and her beauty was clear for all to see. He didn't dare let her know how much he loved her, as it hurt him inside to think how much. Reaching his side, Gytha allowed him to take her hand. All his doubts left him as he bent and kissed her hand. No, Gytha would not use his love to hurt him, it would enrich their life.

Who would have thought that following William to England would bring him to his destiny, and that Gilbert Bayeux would become a married man with such a beautiful wife?

Father Bernard started the marriage service. Gytha could only look up at Gilbert as his grey eyes locked with her beautiful lavender blue ones.

The ceremony was over. Gilbert took Gytha's hand possessively and walked with the small band of guests, Normans and Saxons that had come to terms with the new English king. They were Gunter, who fell in step with Enid, Godfrey and Rolf walking behind them, along with the physician and a few of the higher ranked soldiers.

A feast had been laid out for the villagers and soldiers. The knights and most of the high ranked soldiers went into the main hall.

Gilbert bent and said, 'What now, my Lady Bayeux?' and quickly kissed her gently on the lips. 'Are you not looking forward to tonight?' Gytha blushed and just didn't know how to answer.

Sitting down at the high table, the merrymaking was quickly building as the soldiers began to make lewd remarks to one another.

Gilbert said, 'They are only making merry, some of them have already drank too much ale. Close your ears, my sweet.' Gilbert didn't know that Gytha was so excited inside that she hadn't heard a word with all the noise that was being made. She could only think of how Gilbert had held her when they had walked the night before. Yes, she had liked the feeling of being his. She was sure that once tonight was over, she would be aware of her duties and that Gilbert would be a gentle tutor. Whatever was to happen, she had woven magic images of tonight as she had done as a young girl, and the knight in shining armour had carried her away.

Placing a goblet of wine in her hand, he said, 'Drink a little, my lady. It will relax you for later.' Gytha drank quickly making her cough as it appeared to bubble in her nose. She had not in the past drank much wine. Gytha had usually had a small draft of ale or water with her meals. The wine had been strong and had burnt her throat a little.

Gilbert took a cloth and wiped her mouth, 'Don't be nervous, my little maid, we will manage together. It would be a shame to spoil your beautiful dress. You look so lovely, and I will protect you now and forever.' Taking some meat, he held it to her lips and after she had taken some, he put the rest into his mouth.

They sat and watched the young people merrymaking and playing games. Gunter and Enid had taken Father Bernard to the disputes room to hear their betrothal vows. Enid could not believe that as soon as they possibly could, they would be married. Of course, she realised that Gunter needed to have speech with King William. Suddenly she thought, *what if he says no*. Her dream would then be crushed. She would pray that he would not, and she thought, *God would not let that happen. I have led a blameless life and worked hard.* Yes, herself and Gytha had disobeyed Lord George but only on small things. They hadn't really done anything wrong.

Gilbert was leaning over and speaking to Rolf. Enid leant over and said, 'So, you're a married lady now, my Lady Gytha.'

'It seems so, Enid,' she said with a giggle, having imbibed too much wine. After the first two drinks, she had decided she liked it.

'Pray, what are you two ladies up to?' Gilbert asked as Gunter returned from a trip to the privy. Gytha picked up her goblet to take another drink as she could not control her laughter. Gilbert quickly took it off her.

'I think you have had enough drink, my lady. You will be asleep before we retire, and I wish for you to be awake, 'twill be more enjoyable.'

At this, Gunter could not hold his mirth. 'Perhaps it is time for you to retire, my lord,' he suggested.

'Perhaps! I have decided that you will reside in the solar that I have been using. Enid, you will then be close enough to attend to Gytha until you are wed. If you would like to take your belongings while Gytha and I have a little more time.' He smiled benignly.

'Yes, my lord,' Enid replied with a smile thinking a whole solar to herself! She had always had to share with one sister or another. *How lucky am I*, she thought. In fact, her family resided in the one of the outer round buildings where her sisters had slept in the same room as herself.

'I will help Enid to carry her belongings, my lord, with your permission.'

'You may, Gunter. We will give you time and then my wife and I will retire.' Gunter smiled at Gilbert. 'What, my friend? My lady and I are tired. It's been a long day,' Gilbert said tongue in cheek.

Gunter took Enid's hand and made to leave the hall but not before Rolf and a couple of the older soldiers had made a few suggestive remarks. This brought red spots of colour to Enid's cheeks.

'Take no notice, sweet lady, they have drunk too much ale. They will all have huge headaches in the morning and won't remember a thing,' he laughed. Holding Enid's hand, they made their way to Gytha's chamber. The lewd remarks could still be heard as they went into the passage. 'They mean no harm, Enid. Drink does strange things to a man's brain.'

'Aye, my lord,' she answered for once in full agreement.

Gilbert sat and rubbed his thumb up and down Gytha's hand making her aware that he had to touch her, then lacing his fingers in hers.

'Have we given them enough time, my love?' he asked. Gytha looked into his grey eyes. She was like a rabbit trapped by the eyes of a fox; however, she knew whatever was to happen she wanted to stay trapped. Lord Gilbert was her knight in shining armour, and she wanted to taste the fruits of marriage in his arms. She was Gytha Bayeux and would not want to taste it with any other knight. She had come to the conclusion that whatever it was, she wanted to share it with him.

Standing and taking her hand, he began to thread their way between the merrymaking as soldiers and knights began to suggest different things. Gytha looked up at her new husband in embarrassment. Lifting her up into his arms, he held her close as he pushed through the soldiers that pushed around them. Gytha could smell traces of the soap sweetened by herbs that he had cleansed himself with.

'They mean no harm, my love,' he whispered into her golden hair. 'They are happy for us and are just jesting, sweet lady.' Gytha kept her face buried into his chest.

Gilbert reached the solar and pushed the door open, closing it with his foot. He then placed her down on the floor, saying, 'I'll put the bar down. That will stop anyone thinking that they can bring the jesting to our solar, sweet.'

Looking at her standing there not knowing what to expect, he pulled her to him and gently caressed her face. He kissed her face and neck raising feelings that she wasn't aware that she had. The moment he felt her shudder, he picked her up once more and carried her to the bed. Placing her once more on her feet, he bent and threw a couple of logs on the fire. Gytha noticed that his grey eyes seemed to smoulder with passion. Throwing back the bearskin on the bed, the mattress of straw had been covered in clean linen. He had ordered a serf to attend to this whilst they were merrymaking.

'You won't be able to keep this on, my sweet. It's very pretty, but would be very uncomfortable to lie in,' he said as he took the ring of roses that had formed a coronet on her head. Turning her around and kissing the back of her neck, he gently loosened the laces that held her gown too. She reached back in alarm to stop him, but Gilbert gently captured her hand and murmured strange words to her.

Again, Gilbert continued to loosen her clothing as he held her two hands in one of his, and at the same time pressed her slim form against his. Suddenly, her gown fell to the floor. All he now needed to do was to remove her shift and any other undergarments. First, he had to turn her to face him. Slowly, he kissed her and at the same time pushed her to him.

He hadn't needed to, by now Gytha was his. Her body was feeling strange, and she liked being close to him. Pressing herself closer, she suddenly found herself standing naked in front of him. Guiding her to the bed, he urged her to lie down, and at the same time covered her with the bearskin. Once more kissing her, his eyes never left hers as he began to remove his tunic. Each tight muscle in his chest and stomach rippled with strength as he bent and unlaced the cords on his boots. Gytha let out a gasp as he stood before her as naked as she was.

Carefully removing her hold on the bearskin, he slid into bed beside her, and his hands began to caress her body. Gytha could not help but tremble as he allowed his hands to roam her creamy skin whilst still kissing her neck and the hollow of her throat. What was this strange feeling she felt as she turned and pressed herself to him as she felt that something elusive was waiting for her and what she was not sure? Parting her legs with his, he covered her with his body.

'It will only hurt a little, sweet lady, and after that you will not feel anything, only my love.' Tenderly holding her tight, he made them one suddenly. As she thought that she would find that elusive feeling, he rolled off her still holding her and whispering strange words that seemed to cover her in a cloak of warmth.

'I did not hurt you much, my sweet?' he asked.

''Twas not too hurtful, my lord.'

'Did you enjoy being a married lady? I promise you, it will be better next time,' he whispered.

'It will?' she asked. Once more Gilbert's hands began to stroke her pert breasts, making Gytha tremble with this strange feeling that he teased from the very heart of her.

Gytha had never dreamed that lying with a man would bring such strong feelings from her body as she pressed closer to his roaming hands wanting him to take her once more. This time, Gytha realised that lying with him was enjoyable and exciting, yes it was exciting.

Gilbert groaned as he felt her fulfilment and joined her in the ultimate pleasure of being as one. He decided there and then that he would delay leaving to join William for another day. He would bed his bride for one more night as the thought of leaving her was unbearable. Placing both arms around her, he held her tight to his chest. Gytha would be the only woman in his life now, his one love.

'Sleep now, my little wife. I will always keep you safe by my side.' She was too exhausted to answer.

Snuggling to him, Gytha was soon sound asleep. Her dreams were laced with Gilbert whispering the strange words she needed to learn so she would understand. Both Gytha and Gilbert slept soundly and late for although they had retired early, it had been quite late when they drifted into sleep, both satisfied.

It was a bemused Gilbert that was brought out of his sleep by a banging on the door.

'My Lord Gilbert, wake up! There is a disturbance on the edge of the village. It's a band of renegade soldiers.' Gilbert was out of bed in a flash, quickly throwing on his undergarments. He quickly took the bar off the door.

'What is afoot, Godfrey?'

'There is a band of around thirty renegade soldiers setting fires and trying to overthrow our soldiers on guard. Gunter has gone to rally the other knights and soldiers. I will guard the passage and rally Enid to join our Lady Gytha.'

'You do that, Godfrey, whilst Gytha dresses.'

Looking directly at Gytha, he said, 'Dress warmly, my lady, with a thick cloak. Here is a bag of bread and meat. I feel that you must enter the tunnel and take the bearskin with you. Once Enid is dressed and with you, our Lord Gilbert will furnish you with a couple of rush bundles, one lit to light your way down, but stay within the tunnel and under no circumstances leave it, understand?'

'Tunnel, Godfrey?' Gilbert questioned quickly.

'Time is short, my lord. Whilst I alert Enid, my lady could explain whilst she is dressing. There is no time to spare, my lord. You and I should show our strength as soon as we can.'

Not waiting for Gilbert to answer, he was soon banging on Enid's door who had quickly dressed and unbolted her door.

'Enid, you must join our Lady Gytha in her solar as quickly as you can where she will take you to a safe hiding space until we have quelled this attack. Lady Gytha and Lord Gilbert await you in their solar. Quickly, girl, now.'

Enid was soon fully dressed and entering Gilbert and Gytha's solar. Godfrey had urged her to put on one of the cloaks that Gytha had given to her for warmth. He was now guarding the passage halfway down, his broadsword drawn ready for any intruders to this part of the manor. He would protect his lady and lord to the death.

Gytha had quickly shown Gilbert behind the tapestry. 'This is how you open it, my lord,' Gytha said as she picked up the flagon of ale and bag of bread and meat.

'You didn't see fit to tell me about this little secret, my lady?'

'I would have, my lord, given time. The wedding has been taking the time up.' Giving Gilbert a smile she pre-empted his thoughts, 'I'll never regret that, my lord.'

Gilbert quickly kissed her on the lips. 'You can convince me when we have quelled this little lot.' Enid then entered the solar, three rush bundles in her hand, one lit. Pushing both of them into the passage, Gilbert quickly pushed the bearskin in the passage and then pushed another three rush bundles that already had sheep fat on after them.

'Stay inside, sweet ladies, until we come for you,' were Gilbert's words as he closed the door behind them. Grabbing a short dagger and his broadsword, he was quickly beside Godfrey racing towards the attack. The castle groom had Gilbert's destrier and Godfrey's ready. Already having donned their mail tunics and helmets, both Gilbert and Godfrey were ready for battle. Both men were joined by a number of knights along with Gunter and Rolf.

The band of knights were soon leading a line of soldiers with their shields and broadswords into the battle, and even though they were renegade Norman soldiers, they were no match for Gilbert's well trained Normans that he had led into battle. Gilbert was soon gaining the upper hand once they had beat off the main attack. Gilbert and the knights regrouped and decided that they would route out any that had ridden off to hide in the forest before they fetched Gytha and Enid from their hiding place.

Chapter 15

It took almost two days to beat off the attack. Gilbert knew that he could send Godfrey down the tunnel to check on the Gytha and Enid and take them some more ale and food. They were both reluctant to bring them back into the castle until they knew it was safe and that there would be no more attacks. He would also replenish their stock of rush bundles so they could keep a light burning at all times and another bearskin for extra warmth. Gilbert sent Godfrey back with fresh supplies of food and wine.

Before opening the tunnel, Godfrey placed the bar across the door. Opening the tunnel, he carried a bag of food and wine attached to his belt along with a bearskin over his shoulder and four new bundles of rushes to light. He also left another four at the top. He would tell Enid and Gytha they were there, and they could fetch them if they needed them.

Walking down, he spotted Gytha and Enid halfway down the tunnel. High up in the wall there was a small slit that let a little fresh air in, and there was also an alcove that they had climbed in to make themselves more comfortable.

Giving the extra food and bearskin to Enid, he said, 'Don't leave the tunnel until one of us comes for you, but most of the battle is over. We must just make sure that we have quelled it completely before we bring you out. There are more bundles of rushes not far from the far end if you would like to fetch them, Enid. One of us will try and bring you more supplies if we think you need to stay in here longer. Under no circumstances leave this place, you understand?'

'Yes, Godfrey, we will do as we're told. Go with God, my lord.'

'I will, my lady,' he smiled at Gytha.

'Oh, my Lord Godfrey, tell my Lord Gilbert I am missing him,' she said, going red.

At this point, Enid said, 'If it's a time for declarations, I too miss my Lord Gunter.'

Godfrey shook his head and said, 'My memory is not that good these days, but I will try and remember to pass on your messages.'

'Thank you, my lord,' Gytha said looking at her grandfather's old friend. *I swear*, she thought, *I love him almost as much as I did my grandfather.*

Enid walked down the passage with Godfrey and picked up the rush bundles, 'We will appreciate these extra bundles, my lord. It gives a little warmth and comfort to have the extra bearskin too, thank you, my lord.' Enid turned and left to retrace her steps to Gytha after bidding Godfrey to stay safe.

Gilbert divided the soldiers and churls to guard the manor, arming the churls with bows and arrows. He was certain that they would have all had a little hunting experience when food was short. They would have poached the king's deer here and there to supplement their meat larders. So, most of them could shoot a straight arrow and hit its target.

He made sure that Wally had enough food and meat salted in the kitchen cellars to feed the soldiers, serfs and churls.

As Godfrey made to follow his master to route anyone in the woods, Gilbert said, 'Not you, my old friend. You have the task of looking after Gytha and Enid. You are the only one with the knowledge of where they are.'

Gilbert left Gunter and a band of young knights to guard Alder-Sea. He took with him a small column of soldiers and Rolf who was as strong in his fighting as Gunter. He needed someone as strong as Gunter with him. He was to deal with these renegade Norman soldiers, and each and every one of them would die. He needed to know his manor was safe when he left to join William. He knew William would understand that he could not leave his villagers to marauding soldiers.

With Gilbert at the head of the knights and the soldiers riding behind them, a Norman banner was held aloft by one soldier and another had the banner of Alder-Sea flying above him. Norman and Saxon were together to show their unity.

It wasn't long before Gilbert heard the faint whistle of an arrow speeding towards him. He quickly lunged sideways and the arrow just clinked against his chain mail garment. His quick action had saved his life. When a person had been in as many battles as they had, they were quick to sense arrows as well as hear them. Quickly, he barked orders out and they swerved their column to the side where the arrow had had been aimed from.

Soon Gilbert and his small army were in the midst of a raging battle. Steel clashed with steel and as the Norman soldiers waded into the renegade soldiers, the battle was soon won. Saxon high- ranking officers were to applauded for their courageous fighting.

Not one of the renegade soldiers were spared. The forest floor was strewn with bodies of the unfortunate men. Gunter detailed a group of soldiers to bury the dead. They could not be left to the wolves that lived in the woods. At night, they were sure to be out to feast on the bodies. After all, they were their countrymen, although base and traitorous, they deserved a burial.

Once the burial was completed, the graves were piled with stones to stop animals digging them up. The column searched the woods and made camp as twilight began to creep in. Gilbert would finish his search including the caves come daybreak. Putting guards on the perimeter of the camp, half of the camp settled down to get three hours sleep when they would be woken and the other half would catch some sleep if they could.

As daybreak filtered through the trees and the fingers of light shone against eerie shadows, wild birds were suddenly disturbed on the other side. Gilbert led a number of soldiers to the front whilst another group made their way around the area to cut anyone off who tried to make it back to the caves. Moving quietly, they took the rest of the renegade soldiers by surprise. As some tried to reach the safety of the caves they had left, they were suddenly faced with a line of Norman soldiers and Norman knights. There was no way back. Both renegades and Gilbert's soldiers were tired. Gilbert urged his men forward to show that no one would take advantage of any Saxon or Norman manors whilst he was overlord in this area.

Again, Gilbert made short work of the small band of renegades, and once more the dead were buried. Gilbert had no time for trials that would delay them reaching the north to be by William's side. He still thought there might be more within the caves. Each and every one of them would be searched before he returned to Castle Alder-Sea.

Watching the mouths of the caves so nobody could rush out, a group of soldiers entered the caves to search some with bows already with arrows in place, others with broadswords drawn and still others holding lit torches aloft, enabling them to see in every nook and cranny to ensure they were empty. Most were aware they had dispatched most of the renegade gang.

In one cave, they did find four dirty and hungry soldiers who did nothing to elude capture. They knew that it was useless to fight, and a couple of them were aware who Gilbert was. He was well respected as a fair knight in war and peace and although they knew this, they thought there would only be one ending for their transgressions.

Gilbert recognised one of the younger soldiers who was the son of one of his parents' friends. He was just a boy, and for the life of him he could not understand how he had got involved with this group of hardened criminals. How could he pronounce justice on someone so young? He would take them back to the castle and keep them incarcerated until he was able to have speech with Gunter and Rolf and make some joint decisions. He would wait to make this decision even if it had to be when he returned from serving William.

The rest of the day they spent searching the caves and ensuring that there was no more stragglers. If there were, he did not want them to regroup with other strays inhabiting the forest. Leaving Normans as base as these to join up together again spelt trouble not only to the peaceful villagers but themselves, as they would ruin their own lives. He vowed he had seen enough death. He would look at ways to judge these men. To act in haste could sometimes deliver the wrong decision, and he did not want to take life needlessly. He decided he would find out why they had not joined the others in the attack on the castle.

Gilbert and the knights trooped back through the manor gates, weary and in need of a wash and change of clothing. But first, if it was safe enough, he needed to bring Gytha back to his solar. He had looked into the damp dark tunnel and did not want her or Enid in there longer than necessary. He wanted to hold her in his arms.

The last three days had been an ordeal. He had not wanted to leave anyone alive that could be a threat to Gytha. He had found her and couldn't bear the thought of such men as they had routed out, hurting her or molesting her or any maiden. His life's work now was to make her happy, but it would have to wait until he returned from the north.

Once he was there, he would have to concentrate on fighting the uprising to keep himself safe so that he could return to her safely. As soon as he entered, he asked for Godfrey to be sent to him. He had joined the guard on the bailey to watch for any disturbances.

Godfrey was soon entering his solar, 'You wished to see me, my lord,' he asked.

'Yes, Godfrey, tell me, do you think it's safe enough to bring my Lady Gytha back inside with Enid? I imagine it's quite cold in there overnight.'

'It should not be a problem, my lord. We will be on our guard and can always return them back if we feel there is any danger, Lord Gilbert.'

'Let us place the bar across the door and fetch them back in before they freeze to death or starve,' Gilbert said. He was quite tired, but all he wanted to do was sleep for a short while. He was almost asleep on his feet, since he hadn't slept for the last two days. And at least with a good number of soldiers on guard, both he and the others could catch up on their sleep.

First, he must have Gytha back beside him which would help him to sleep. He thought of her and Enid in that cold, dark tunnel, and he felt they would both be safer by his and Gunter's company. As Godfrey had suggested, they could always go back into the tunnel if there was any immediate danger.

Godfrey was by now putting the bar across the door.

'Tell me, Godfrey, is this the only such tunnel in the manor or are there more?' he said as he helped Godfrey re-locate the door behind the tapestry.

'There is another, my lord, at the far end of the passage under the steps to the bailey. It is some time since it has been used, so it would be awkward to open.'

'Well, Godfrey, we have no need of it at the moment and the location need to stay with us that know they are there. If too many are made aware of them, they could become of no use when we need them.'

'I understand, my lord,' came Godfrey's reply. He too thought it was prudent to keep these tunnels a secret or they became useless.

Passing Gilbert a lit rush bundle, he said, 'They are around halfway down the tunnel in a small alcove in the wall, my Lord Gilbert. I will stay here and make sure no one comes to the door and thinks it strange that it's unoccupied and the door is barred.'

'You have done well, Godfrey, and thought of everything. I will bring them back quickly. Build the fire, my good man, they are bound to be cold.'

'I will also put water to heat, sir. I'm sure they will both wish to wash after the time spent in that tunnel.'

Gilbert smiled his thanks and made his way along the musty dark tunnel. As he walked along, he thought it was a good escape route for family but to stay in this tunnel for almost three days was most objectionable for a man, never mind maidens. At least it had kept them out of harm's way while the short skirmish had been sorted.

At last, he came upon the small alcove that Enid and Gytha had placed their bearskins and small number of supplies.

As Gilbert held aloft his light to locate them, Gytha sat up and unmistakably cried excitedly, 'Gilbert!' and scrambled to him in her haste to get to him. He held her tightly to him. He too felt the loss of her company for the last two days. How he would manage without her when he joined William, he didn't know, but manage he would have to.

'Come, Enid, let's get you both warm,' he said, realising that in his relief of holding each other he and Gytha had forgotten the other maid's presence. Taking the bearskins in his arms, he urged Enid to pick up the flagons that had held the wine, thinking it would be a good idea to keep some corked ale in this passage along with a box holding bundles of rushes and some sheep fat in a container to ensure they had ready lighting down there.

Urging Enid and Gytha in front of him, holding the light aloft so that all three of them could see the way back to the solar, they would soon be warm. He and Godfrey could see to the fire in Enid's solar while the two maids washed and dressed in clean clothes. He would make sure Wulf slept outside the two solars that night in case of further disturbance, but he thought that would not be the case. Gilbert would not leave anything to chance now. He would make sure that the Castle Alder-Sea was left well-guarded and that some of the churls were trained to sword and bow until he returned.

'Godfrey and I will just go and make sure your fire in your solar is burning bright, Enid, and in the mean-time, Gytha, you can freshen up. It's not been pleasant for you in that tunnel, and we'll also get Wulf to bring you fresh food from the kitchens. I'm sure you will both benefit from that. Don't forget to bar the door, sweet lady,' he said, reaching for Gytha and kissing her quickly. Saxons would not be so keen to show their feelings with others present, but Gilbert could not help himself. He ached for her already. How was he going to manage the time he would be away? He would have to, he thought.

Turning on their heel, Gilbert and Godfrey left to make sure that Enid's fire was attended to and that Wulf would fetch food for them, instructing him to give them a little time before carrying it to the solar. Making a last check on the guard to ensure they were adequately guarded for the night, he walked to Godfrey's solar with him and wished him a good night's rest.

Enid busied herself helping Gytha to strip off her soiled clothing. The two girls had gone to the far end of the corridor and used it for a privy as far away from where they had been resting as they could. Both felt the need to wash once they were back inside the solar. Enid helped Gytha with her water and kept hot water coming until Gytha was completely clean without using the tin bath.

Helping Gytha into a clean shift, she said, 'I will go back to my own solar, Gytha. My Lord Gilbert might be back sooner than you think. It was obvious he missed you.'

Gytha looked at her old friend, her face blushing pink, 'Aye, I missed him too, Enid. I will ask Wulf, who is sure to bring food, to bring some to your solar. By then, you should have washed and be ready to eat.'

'Yes, I'll be ready for some fresh bread and meat. Sleep well, Gytha, I will see you in the morning, and you will be much rested then.'

'You too, my friend,' came Gytha's answer as she watched Enid enter her solar, waving as she entered.

Turning back to her solar, she closed the door and sat in one of the chairs by the fire to await Gilbert. A small scratching came on the door, and Gytha bid them to enter. It was Wulf carrying a laden tray.

'My Lord Gilbert bid me tell you that he will soon join you. I will put the food out for you and my Lord Gilbert and put it nearer to the fire for you. I will now be outside the solar if you need anything.'

'Thank you, Wulf. I'm certain we will have enough, goodnight.'

Gytha waited nervously for Gilbert to return. Suddenly, the door opened, and Gytha stood up quickly. Within a couple of strides, Gilbert was by her side, pulling her to him. He buried his lips in her hair.

'Sweet lady, I have missed you so much,' he whispered, holding her tight.

She gently pushed him away and said, 'Your food, my lord. There is plenty of time for speech after you eat.' Gilbert smiled and led her to the table. Sharing a trencher, they sat and ate in companiable silence.

'Come, my lady, it's time to retire,' he said with a smile. They both washed their hands in a finger bowl that Wulf had placed on the table.

Standing by the bed after they had washed, Gilbert held her close, gently teasing her senses and his hands undoing the strings to her shift, letting it slip to the floor as he did with her dress. Pulling off his tunic, he picked her up and laid her on the bed. Walking around the solar, he snuffed out the rush bundles after he had put more logs on the fire. Taking off the rest of his clothes, he slid into bed beside Gytha, pulling her close to him. Turning, she clung to him.

'Sweet lady,' he whispered as he took her to him.

That night was peaceful. They both slept contentedly as Gilbert held her protectively in his arms. Morning was soon on them, and Gilbert got out of bed and put on his undergarments and built up the fire to make sure the solar was warm for Gytha. He even hung the can over the fire to heat for Gytha to wash. He himself made do with cold water, and it was quite invigorating.

Gytha lay watching him from the bed. Why had she been so frightened of being wed? If everyone was like Gilbert, they would never be frightened. He was such a loving, gentle husband.

Walking over to the bed, he leant over her and kissed her lips. 'How is my beautiful wife this morning? Hungry, I presume.'

Gytha smiled back, 'Yes, my lord, I am.'

'Well, you busy yourself having a wash while I send Wulf to the kitchens to bring some food. Then I hate to leave you even while I inspect the castle perimeters to ensure everything is safely guarded.' Kissing her quickly, he went in search of Wulf to send him for food for them to break their fast. As he went down the corridor, he bumped into Gunter coming in search of him.

'You look better for your sleep, if you slept at all, Gilbert,' he said jokingly.

'You wait until you are wed to Enid. You will understand, my friend,' he smiled back.

'Well, I have done the rounds and the night has been quiet, and there are no problems. Everything is peaceful.'

'Well, that means I can join my beautiful wife to break my fast now. Have you visited Enid, Gunter?'

'I did last night but alas I have to wait until I'm wed to receive any favours,' he laughed.

'So you should. I will re-join Gytha. If you see Wulf, ask him to bring our food from the kitchens to break our fast,' Gilbert laughed back.

'I already have. I was just about to tell you your food is on its way, my friend.'

'Thank you, Gunter. After we have broken our fast, we must make plans to ensure that Alder-Sea and all that reside here are safe while we are absent with King William. We must make sure at all costs.'

'Yes, we must, Gilbert. I will tell Rolf and Godfrey if you wish. Say in about an hour, my friend?'

'Yes, in the disputes room,' came Gilbert's answer.

Gilbert turned and both men went their separate ways, Gilbert making his way back to Gytha in their solar. Striding back in, he lifted her off her feet.

'Our food will be here soon, then I have a meeting to attend with Godfrey, Gunter and Rolf, my love, so perhaps Enid will be up and about and you can keep each other company for the rest of the morning.'

'You will be back after, my lord?' Gytha asked shyly.

'I will, my sweet. I hate to leave you at all but the safety of our manor has to be one of our priorities,' came his quiet answer. She still did not know that in a couple of days they would have to leave to join William, although she had known he would be going. It would be a wrench at their heart strings for both of them, as he was sure that Gytha loved him as he did her.

Gytha watched the door close behind him. Enid would soon be in to keep her company. For once, Gytha would have preferred Gilbert's company. There was so much that she did not know about this man, and she could not understand how quickly he had become important to her. She felt safer with him around. She would have liked to go to the meeting with him and was very aware that what he was to plan would be a man's work and that she would have to accept.

Enid was soon knocking on the door, and she bid her to enter. Enid was as welcome as ever. Enid was bursting with excitement. Gilbert had sent the young soldier back to William's camp with a message that Alder-Sea had been under attack and would be joining him within a week. He had also sent a message asking William to grant permission for Gunter's request to marry Enid. He was also happy to say if William agreed, then he, Gilbert Bayeux, was happy for the union to take place.

He explained to William that he needed to leave Gunter behind to help Gytha and to protect the villagers with a small band of soldiers. Gilbert would bring Rolf and some of the younger knights along with the remaining soldiers to fight alongside William. As Gunter was to stay behind, they would send someone back to give Gunter William's answer, then he and Enid would perhaps be able to wed.

'You don't think he will say no to us, do you, Gytha?' Enid asked worriedly.

'Take heart, Enid. Why would he? It's obvious that he knows all of Gunter's attributes, and he values him as he values Gilbert. You too could enjoy being a married lady, Enid,' Gytha smiled at her friend.

'Will you advise me of how to act?'

'I won't need to, for there is nought to it. Leave that part to Gunter,' said Gytha with a smug smile. Both girls broke into peals of laughter for they both knew how worried Gytha had been at her own lack of experience in the bed chamber.

Chapter 16

Gilbert sent Wulf to the solar to see if Gytha and Enid would like some refreshment and to tell them that Lord Gilbert wished for them to stay within the solar until suppertime. He and Gunter would come for them. Gilbert, Gunter, Rolf and several other young knights were planning the protection of Alder-Sea while they were away, and of course, tomorrow they would do another sweep of the forest and caves to make sure there were no more renegades hiding within them.

Once in the complaints room he said to Gunter, 'One of my father's old friend's son is with the prisoners we took from the cave, young Fredrick Allman. I feel that he might enlighten us why they were hiding in the cave, and after that, we will separate them to see if they come up with the same answer.'

'You think that they realised they had involved themselves with the wrong side?'

'I feel that he might not have had the stomach to attack. They surrendered without a fight.'

'You could be right, Gilbert,' came Gunter's thoughtful reply.

'Methinks that they were more frightened of the renegade soldiers they had joined than us. Separate them and don't give them time to talk of why they were sent for. I might then pardon them and take them back to battle with us in William's name. But first, let us see what they have to say for themselves.'

'You want Fredrick first, Gilbert?'

'I think so. He will, I think, be truthful to myself. He knew who I was.'

'Right, I will give orders to separate them before they can come up with any untruths, and then bring Fredrick in.' Gilbert smiled his thanks and awaited Gunter's return with the first prisoner.

It wasn't long before he returned with Fredrick flanked by four soldiers. Stepping back so that they were in a line behind the young soldier, Gilbert stayed quiet as he scrutinised the young man who looked Gilbert in the eyes, his gaze not wavering.

Leaning forward, Gilbert said, 'Well, what have you to say for yourself?' His voice held an edge of steel whilst his eyes never left Fredrick's face. He wanted to be aware of every movement the young soldier made.

Clearing his throat, Fredrick said, 'I can only say that we knew we had done wrong. It was adventure we wanted, not killing and raping maids. Some of us did not think our actions through before leaving William's side until it was too late. I will make no excuses, my lord. I will take my punishment, I hope bravely. You know my father would agree with whatever you decide. He would bear no ill-will towards you. I have dishonoured my father's name, and I can only say I deserve it.'

'Why were you and the others not with the group that attacked us, boy?' Gilbert rapped out.

'We not only deserted William in a time of madness, but we also deserted the soldiers that led us to do so. We were hiding in the caves from them hoping to escape and return to William's side if possible.'

'You speak truth, boy?'

'By the Holy Mother, I do, my lord.'

Turning to the guards, he said, 'Take him to a holding place and don't allow him to speak to the other prisoners, and Gunter, bring in the next prisoner.'

'I will,' Gunter replied, walking behind the soldiers guarding the prisoner making sure that he was housed in another part of the guardhouse unable to have speech with any of the others.

Each and every one of the soldiers were quite young and gave the same answer to the questions that Gilbert rapped out. From what he could see, they had been tempted away with the same promises by a group of older and much harder soldiers with their eye on gain and women. They would not fight fairly and would attack manors that they thought might not be protected so well. They had not realised that Alder-Sea had now a Norman overlord and that it was well protected.

Once they had all been interviewed, Gilbert decided that it would do them good to cool off for another night.

He turned to Gunter and said, 'Come, let us all prepare for supper. We can discuss our next step tomorrow.'

'Yes, Gilbert, it will do them good to sweat for another night. They did all have the same reason for hiding in the cave, although they used different speech.'

'Yes,' was the only word that Gilbert uttered. Gunter bid leave of Gilbert, asking him if he would kindly advise Enid that he would return to escort her to supper. Opening the door to the solar, Enid and Gytha were still laughing.

'Well, sweet ladies, what is all this merriment about? Could you share the joke with me?' he asked, a puzzled expression on his face.

Enid went red, 'No, my lord!' she answered, 'it's maid talk. I better leave you to prepare for supper,' once more having composed herself.

'Enid, Gunter bid me to tell you that he will call for you to escort you to supper.'

'Thank you, my lord,' she said letting out a sigh of relief. She had expected him to be angry with them, 'twas after all just a little bit of fun. Now she thought she needed to be a little more in control of herself when Gilbert was around. After all, it 'twas just fun.

Once Enid left, Gilbert walked over to Gytha and pulled her to her feet. Holding her tight against him he said, 'We must get ready for supper, my love,' but continued to hold her tight. He would lie with her now, but he would be expected to be in the main hall with his knights and soldiers so it would have to wait.

'Yes, my lord,' she whispered against his chest. She too appeared not to want to move away from him.

Reaching for a fresh tunic, he asked, 'Have you washed, my love?'

'Yes, my lord.'

Gilbert held her slightly away from him, 'Say my name, Gytha. It's Gilbert, we are wed.'

Pushing back into his arms, she whispered, 'Gilbert.'

'That wasn't hard, was it? Now get dressed, and we can have supper and be back early if you wish so.'

She reached for a fresh gown and turned to look at him. She answered clearly, 'I do wish, Gilbert,' as her face flushed pink. The smile that he gave Gytha was full of promise realising they had all night together. How he would miss his beautiful wife. He hoped it would not take too long, and he would be back. Opening his solar door and leading Gytha out, they were just in time. Gunter was knocking on Enid's door. All four of them strolled into the main hall to take their place at the high table.

The food as usual was well cooked and varied, and they all ate their fill. Gilbert poured Gytha a goblet of wine and made sure he had enough meat and pie on their trencher to satisfy both of them, although Gytha had never had a huge appetite which was why she was so slim and graceful.

Gytha washed her hands in the finger bowl, and Gilbert instantly washed his and held her hand. He wanted to be close to her as much as possible until he left.

Tomorrow, he would hold court in the disputes room. He would have Gytha present at his side as she needed to be aware of his ways and judgements along with the running of the manor. He would also head a hunting party tomorrow to make sure that the stores were full of meat and supplies to feed them all if they needed to stay close to the manor and to make sure that someone salted the meat and that they had plenty of grain and veg in the cellars. He trusted Gunter to look after his wife for the time he was with William; however, she needed to be aware that she was head of manor and to look to Gunter and Godfrey in his absence.

'We won't dally too long, my sweet. You need to join me for part of the judgements in the complaints court tomorrow and to be part of the plans.' Gytha was young whilst he was in his thirty third year of life. She needed to learn more about the running of the manor. Godfrey would be here along with Gunter to protect her. She must be seen as the head of the manor, and act accordingly.

He smiled to himself. The way that she and Enid had been laughing gave him an insight into the fact that she had not grown up until she lay with him. Gytha needed a little responsibility to help her to understand the role of his wife. Whatever she did do, he knew she could do no wrong in his eyes. Even though they had cemented their vows by coupling, she still looked at him with eyes that were innocent.

After supper, Gilbert and Gunter escorted Gytha and Enid back to the solar. 'Perhaps Enid would like to keep you company for a short while as Gunter and I need to make some plans for hunting tomorrow and the complaints court. I wish for you to attend that part with myself and my trusted friends. I will be back soon, my sweet,' Gilbert said.

Gunter bent and kissed Enid's hand. 'Until tomorrow, sweet lady,' he whispered. Enid blushed prettily.

'Goodnight, my lord,' she whispered. She could not wait to be the same as Gytha, a married lady. Then he would not leave her by the door. Both maids went into the solar, and Gytha quickly pulled off the coif covering her hair and ran her fingers through her golden curls. Pulling the chairs closer to the fire, they settled down to a chat.

It was quite late when Gilbert arrived back at the solar. They had spent the last few hours putting in plans for tomorrow and making sure that everything was fully stocked if they had to manage without extra food gathering. It wasn't likely, but Gilbert was methodical in his approach to ensure their safety at the manor, and Gunter was well schooled in his ways. He would be leaving his family and the manor in a safe pair of hands.

Sitting down in the chair that Enid had vacated, he reached for Gytha's hand. 'Are you happy, my lady?'

'Yes, my lord, I didn't think I would be,' she whispered, 'but I am.'

'Well, I think it's time we retired, my love.' Gytha was still shy, and Gilbert moved around the solar and put out the rush bundles that lit the solar. Gilbert gave Gytha a few minutes to undress as he built up the fire to make sure the solar was warm. He then undressed in the firelight. Gytha watched his every move as he undressed taking in his firm body. He was so strong, and she could already imagine his arms around her. She revelled in the fact that this knight was her wedded husband. Soon he was lying beside her, holding her. Contentment washed over her as they drew close.

Chapter 17

Gytha stirred in Gilbert's arms. He had lain watching her for the last half hour, and his finger was tracing the contours of her face as she had slept. Opening those startling blue eyes, she smiled at him.

He kissed her and said, 'I would verily prefer to stay here, but I'm afraid both of us will be busy this morning. We are to hunt this afternoon, so you must make haste and wash. I will wash first then there will be some warm water for you.' He climbed out of bed and stirred the fire to flame more. He threw some logs on and hung the water to warm whilst he washed. Gytha once more watched him unashamedly as he doused himself with cold water.

Pulling on his tunic and leggings, he sat lacing his moleskin boots, his eyes on her perfect body as she cleansed herself and splashed some rose water on her body. She went to reach for a clean shift, and as she did so, Gilbert passed her one with a smile. She hadn't thought about the fact that she was walking about naked. Quickly, she climbed into her underclothes and chose a dress of a gold material that Gilbert had brought back with her wedding gown.

Once her dressing was finished, the kitchen hand brought food for them to break their fast. Gilbert went to the chest and took out a chain of office slightly smaller than his, showing clearly the Bayeux symbol. It was made of gold and had diamonds around her and Gilbert's initials.

'No one will wonder who you are, my lady, with that around your neck.'

'Why it's beautiful, Gilbert,' she said looking at him in amazement. He had already gifted her with presents when they had wed. Finding a coif for her hair, she was ready.

Looking at him, she commented, 'I wonder how long it will take my hair to grow. Grandfather cropped it to make me look like Guy.'

'To me, Gytha, you have always looked beautiful even when you were Guy. It would be nice to see it grow long though. You must grow it again. Your grandfather, as you said, was only trying to protect you, so take heart. It will soon grow again.'

'You are right, Gilbert, it will soon grow.'

'Come, my love, we must away to the chamber of complaints. We must make some decisions on a small matter that Gunter and I investigated yesterday.' Holding his hand out, he waited for her to place her hand into his and led her into the passage to make their way to the small chamber used for complains and trials.

Walking into the chamber, Gytha noticed that where her grandfather's chair was situated there were now two. Leading Gytha onto the dais, he seated her on his right side putting a footstool under her small feet for comfort. He then sat in her grandfather's chair. Gunter, Rolf and a number of younger knights flanked them. There was the sergeant of the guard and several soldiers standing by the door.

'Bring in the prisoners,' Gilbert instructed. Gytha immediately looked at him. What was he going to do? She had imagined that it would just be the normal complaints that cropped up, usually warring farmers who had a grudge with each other. She was even more amazed when they marched back with a group of boys that looked no older than Wulf.

Gilbert looked at them and said, 'You are here because you acted in a way that amounted to treason. By rights you should be stripped of your standing as Norman soldiers and hung.'

Gytha immediately jumped up. 'But Gilbert, they are just boys like Guy was. 'Tis not right, they are too young.' Gilbert held his hand up to stop her speech, then relented a little as he saw the stricken look in her eyes.

Turning to her and smiling, he said, 'Not quite like Guy, sweet lady,' his voice soft and low as he addressed her. Holding her gaze, he said, 'Why, what would you do with deserters, Gytha?'

'Well, what have they done that is so wrong, my lord?'

'They deserted William's army to follow renegade soldiers. What would you do?'

'Everyone deserves a second chance, my lord, if they are suitably sorry. Perhaps William would welcome them back if they have done naught that is too wrong, and besides, even I have disobeyed Grandfather by going into the woods and caves to play with Enid, Wulf and others when we were children and had been warned not to. Grandfather did not hang any of us.'

At this, Gilbert smiled, 'You have a pretty way of putting your argument forward, my love, but it is the way I was thinking. What do you think, Gunter, Rolf?'

'My Lady Gytha is right, my lord. She thinks a little like you.'

'What have you to say for yourselves?' Gilbert asked the young men.

One of the young men spoke up, 'You asked why we were hiding in the caves, and I think we all might have told you the same. We had our head turned by hardened soldiers and were not aware of what we were doing, the enormity of what we have done. Having our heads turned and being promised maids sounded good. I, for one, would prefer to fight and die for William than on the other end of a rope.'

'What say all of you? Will you kneel at my feet and swear loyalty to myself and lady Gytha? Norman and Saxon blood united?'

'Aye!' the young men said in unity.

'Then so be it. You will kneel and swear loyalty. Then you will be taken to the armoury to bathe and put on clean clothes; however, you will have an older soldier who you will be attached to. They will be your mentor. One step out of line and the rope will be yours.' The relief on the young men's faces was clear for all to see.

Bowing their heads, they said, 'Thank you, my lord.' Each and every one one kneeled and swore loyalty.

'You will return with myself and the other soldiers to William's side in the north where we must take up arms in his name. We only fight to bring peace and don't make war on innocent people, is that clear?'

'Yes, my lord,' their answer came in unity.

As everyone dispersed, Gilbert stood and advised Gytha, 'I will see you back to our solar, my lady. Wulf will bring you a drink, then myself, Gunter, and a small band of soldiers intend to do a little hunting to fill our stores to ensure we have plenty of venison and such salted for a while. I will be back to join you for supper, my sweet.' Taking her hand, he guided her back to the solar. 'Perhaps Enid would like to join you for a drink. You may take a walk in the grounds if you wish but do not venture outside, my lady.'

'Yes, Gilbert,' she answered demurely.

'Until later, my sweet,' he said, leaving her at the door of her solar. He banged on Enid's door as he passed. Enid quickly opened it to see Gilbert walking away and Gytha waiting in their doorway. Enid followed Gytha into the solar.

'We can have a drink and then take a walk after if you've a mind to, Enid, but only in the manor grounds. Like Grandfather, he has warned me not to wander outside.'

Enid smiled. 'Aye and unlike Grandfather we must obey him. I fear I would not want to spend too long in the tunnel. It smells so musty.'

'Yes, I swear I can still smell it in my nostrils' it stays with me.' At that moment, Wulf arrived with a flagon of wine. 'Thank you, Wulf. Come and have a drink with us. Has Gilbert given you any task to do?' queried Gytha.

'No, my lady.'

'Then you can have a drink with us and join us on our walk. The fresh air will do us good.'

'I'd like that, my lady,' came his answer.

'There was a time that you both called me Gytha. I haven't changed. I'm still your friend, and yes, Gilbert might want you to address me as my lady, but when we are together, Gytha is my name.'

Enid lifted her goblet. 'To us, friends forever.' From then and for the two hours spent in the garden, they reminisced on childhood games. It had been an uncomplicated period in their life, and all three cherished their memories.

Enid helped Gytha to collect a bunch of early rosebuds to put in her solar. She urged Enid to do the same. Wulf gallantly carried the flowers for them. They stood and watched Gilbert, Gunter and Rolf alight from horses laden with game that had been shot and birds as well, even wild boar. They had certainly been very busy that day.

'Come, we will return. Gilbert will want to freshen up before he takes supper. Wulf, will you fetch a fresh flagon of wine so that he can drink before supper?'

'Yes, Gytha,' he said smiling, returning to the main hall with the two girls. The two girls parted at the solar door promising to see each other at supper.

Gytha quickly hung garments up and placed water to heat before Gilbert arrived at the door. She had been a little lazy and had chosen to walk with Enid in the gardens, leaving feminine garments not hung up. Gilbert was very tidy. She had noticed how he placed his laundry at once, not having to sort at a later date. Gytha had now taken note of his tidiness and was trying hard not to be untidy. As a small girl, someone had always fetched and carried for her. She made a mental note that she would not leave everything to the serfs. Had she not seen to the fresh rushes for the floor and placing the sweet herbs amongst them to freshen the room when she had been Guy? Gytha had liked the feeling of looking after Grandfather, and she was sure that she enjoyed looking after Gilbert.

By the time Gilbert returned to the solar, Gytha had managed to complete the tasks that needed to be completed. She had spread fresh rushes and put away clothes. The sweet herbs that were quickly sprinkled by herself on the top had freshened the air of daily living. She had already washed and sat in her shift with a cloak over the top ready to put on a fresh gown for supper. The door opened, and Gilbert sat down. Gytha rose from her chair to pore a goblet of wine for him.

'To refresh you, Gilbert,' she said a pink glow on her cheeks, partly because she had quickly attended to her duties. Gilbert caught her hand and pulled her down to sit on his knee, holding her tight on his arm as he drank deeply. His one thought was that he would soon be leaving her not knowing when he would return. Draining his glass, he picked her up and carried her to the bed. Placing her down, he went and put the bar against the door before joining her with a sigh of contentment on the bed.

It was sometime later that he spoke, 'We had better have another wash, my sweet, or we won't be eating supper tonight. We have dallied long enough.' He got up, but she stayed where she was watching him pour water into the bowl quickly. His muscles rippled in the firelight as he washed. Then he filled the bowl with more warm fresh water for Gytha to wash. As he dressed, he watched Gytha's every movement. If truth be told, he would have liked to have stayed on the bed holding her close. Gilbert knew that he would have to return Gytha to the solar after supper, as he would be kept late making more plans to ensure the safety of the manor. After the last two hours together, he was sure she would be too tired to wait up for his return. He knew that if he so wished, he could wake her, but he knew he would not disturb her slumber.

Once Gytha had dressed in a blue silk dress and used her favourite rose water, they were ready to take supper. Enid and Gunter were waiting outside of Enid's solar.

'You are ready at last, Gilbert. I trust you have rested?' said Gunter, greeting him with a cheeky grin. Gilbert just smiled and chose not to answer. His good friend knew him too well.

Gilbert and Gunter's speech quickly changed to business as they walked to the main hall. They had a lot of areas to cover in the next two days. The attack on the manor had delayed their return to William's side, and he knew that William would understand why it took a little longer to re-join him. For him, the last few days had been heaven. He realised that he and Gytha had a special affinity to each other that distance could not break. All the same, the call back to William's side had been much too soon. They would have to fight twice as quick to return him back to Gytha's side.

Supper once more had many varied dishes. Gunter, Rolf and Gilbert were distracted by business and talked of the approaching journey back to William. Gunter could see the merit in being left behind to advise and help to protect Alder-Sea along with Godfrey. He was slightly older than Rolf, and they were both Gilbert's good friends. He was more outgoing than Rolf who was quieter by nature. He could always come up with excellent war strategy. Gilbert had already a plan in mind for Rolf. He had decided that when he returned that Rolf too needed a wife, and Rolf had been especially fond of his sister. Who knows, he or Gunter could be granted lands. If so, they needed a strong family around them. He had a maid in his mind for him, but it would wait. He would send a message home whilst in the north; it could bear fruit.

Turning to Gytha, he said, 'I'm afraid that I must once again have speech with my trusted friends and loyal soldiers so when you have had your supper, I must return you to our solar. If you wish, you may wait up for me unless you are tired. Either way, I will try to be back to your side quickly.'

'I will look forward to your return, Gilbert,' she said her face blushing and her dimple showing making Gilbert's heart beat faster knowing that she was as willing as him to lie together. With a smile, he grasped her hand, and Gunter and he escorted their two ladies back to their solars. Bending his head, he took Gytha's lips. She kissed him back eagerly, once more making his heart beat with longing to be joining her in the solar at that moment.

Turning quickly to see that Gunter had said his goodnights to Enid, he hoped that William's answer came back quickly for Gunter's sake. He had never seen his good friend so patient to bed a maid but, he, Gilbert Bayeux, could see the merit of waiting until wed. In fact, Gunter had always been one step of him in persuading a maid to sleep with him.

It had been quite late when Gilbert returned to the solar. He found Gytha asleep in the chair. In her hands she held one of Gilbert's undergarments that needed stitching, and the needle was still in her hand. Gilbert gently moved the garment and needle from her hands and carried her to the bed. There he began to remove her gown. Leaving her shift on, he placed her under the bearskin. Putting more logs onto the fire to keep the chamber warm, he doused the rush bundles that lit the solar. Standing and undressing in the firelight, he pulled her close into his arms. He could be patient until the morning, he thought with a sigh, he too was tired.

Chapter 18

Gytha awoke to the gentle stroking of her body by Gilbert. Putting her arms around his neck, she pulled him to her. He didn't need to be invited twice as they blended as one. He knew he had not long in her bed before he had to take up arms. He had lingered here longer than he should have. Still, it was a good thing that he had delayed leaving by the couple of days, who knows what would have happened at Alder-Sea if they had not. At least this way they had made arrangements that Alder-Sea was better protected, and he had left more soldiers behind to fortify the castle and its lands.

He would have this one last night, for tomorrow he needed to lead a column of knights and soldiers back to fight. Gilbert was sure that he had left the strongest knight, Gunter, to protect his home and family.

He was quiet as they broke their fast. Gytha hoped that it wasn't that she hadn't pleased him. He had appeared well satisfied, after, *yes, he was,* she thought, *don't doubt yourself.* She knew he brought the woman out in her; in fact, he made her feel wanton. She wasn't sure it was seemly to want him so much. She knew she liked being a married lady, and she had nought to fear of marriage, she had found.

'Will you walk with me a little before I need to get down to business with Godfrey, Gunter and a few of the others?'

'I would enjoy that, Gilbert.' Holding her hand, he chose to walk around the village to speak to the churls and bond men. This way, they would see him with their Lady Gytha happy and contented as a married lady. This would also help to keep the villagers loyalty to not only Gytha but himself.

He already knew he needed some extra help in the manor so because the seamstress was now a widow, he elevated her to housekeeper to help Gytha, and she would reside in the servants' quarters within the manor. Gytha was pleased with his choice. She had as a little girl received sweet treats from the good lady.

Once they had done a complete walk of the village, Gilbert had to go to oversee his business with his chosen knights and soldiers. Then tonight he needed to tell Gytha that he would be leaving to follow William to take up arms. He wondered how she would take it. He had found her a passionate wife despite her knowing naught of wifely duties in the bed chamber. Would he have to remind her that he was the only man she must lie with?

'I will take a walk in the rose garden, Gilbert, if you don't mind.'

'No, my love, I don't. It will be suppertime before I join you. We have a lot to discuss. You can look at the flowers in the garden, but you won't find a sweeter rose, or more beautiful one than you,' he said lifting her hand to his mouth and kissing it.

Gytha spent another hour wandering the garden. The smell of the roses was strong. Being careful not to scratch her hands on the thorns, she carefully picked a bunch of red and deep pink roses to put in a container in the solar. The perfume was so strong it would be sure to cheer the solar up whilst helping it to smell sweet.

Gytha carried her precious bunch of flowers to her solar placing them into a spare wooden jug. She placed them on a little table and was pleased with the effect. She also noticed that someone had been in and changed the rushes on the floor and generally tidied her clothing up, and the clothes for the wash house had gone. She really had meant to do it herself. Once more, Enid or Wulf had beat her to it. She had lingered too long amongst the roses when going for a walk and taking in all the sweet smells of each flower. She would do better. She felt that since her dear grandfather had passed, she had grown up immensely. It was only natural that she would, but of course, she still had to work on it.

Putting more logs on the fire, Gytha freshened up and awaited Gilbert's return. She had noticed that part of the morning he had been preoccupied. Gytha worried about what was making him so. She looked at her stitching bag. She would keep herself occupied with continuing to repair Gilbert's clothes that needed attending to.

This was how Gilbert found her, concentrating on the work in the bag. She hadn't been one for sewing but intended to come to terms with it. She wanted Gilbert to see she wanted to be a good wife and look after him.

'What have you there?' said Gilbert as he entered the solar. 'Not more sewing?' he said smiling at her endeavours.

'I do declare, Gilbert, it's not my favourite pastime, my lord, but I will master it and show you that I will make a good wife.'

Kneeling at her feet, Gilbert declared, 'You are the best wife anyone could wish for; in fact, we have just about enough time to lie a little together,' he said picking her up and depositing her on the bed. There was a quick coupling on the bed, then he quickly pulled her up after and taking the water that she had kept warm, they washed quickly. They needed to attend supper, and they only just made their dressing before Gilbert and Enid were at the door.

Gunter was usually full of banter but not tonight. Half of him wanted to follow his friend to take up arms, and the other wanted to stay by his dear Enid. He was finding it hard not to persuade her to lie with him. He would to the best of his ability ensure that he protected his good friend's home and wife until he returned. He would miss both Rolf and Gunter, for the friendship of the three knights went deep, and each one would have liked to stay together. This was not always possible, but they would all be back at Alder-Sea after the battle was over, God willing.

Suppertime was quieter than most nights as some of the soldiers were aware that they too would follow their Lord Gilbert to William's side. There was always an element that they might not return as battles could be hard. Camping in all weather, slipping and sliding in mud, it was fair to say that some of the soldiers would prefer staying at Alder-Sea as it was quite comfortable, more than being in the thick of fighting, and they had not realised that it would be just a short time before they would be fighting once more.

It was the fault of the fledgeling Edgar that some Saxons thought was his right. William up until now had been patient with the young Edgar but now he was stretching William's patience. William released that he must put an ending to this latest claim. He himself wanted to settle in England and raise one of his sons to inherit the throne when he had expired.

As Gilbert escorted Gytha back to the solar, he stepped inside. He held her close for a moment and whispered, 'The time has come, my love. I have to re-join William tomorrow, and I hate to leave you when I have had such a short time with you. I will be back. You must not lose heart.'

'Must you, Gilbert? Can't you stay and Gunter join William instead?' she said selfishly.

'No, my sweet. I above all have to go as William has requested that I lead my comrades into battle, perhaps it won't be too long.'

'I will miss you so,' Gytha said, her lavender blue eyes filling with tears and escaping down her cheek.

'I will miss you too, sweet lady. Time will soon pass. You have Godfrey to protect you, and Enid can move back into our solar until I return, although I feel it won't be long before she shares Gunter's solar as they will wed.'

'You think, my lord?'

'I do, sweet lady, and I know it will please you.'

'Yes, I will be pleased for her. As you say, she's my very good friend.'

'Promise you won't retire tonight until I return, my love. It's our last night for a time.'

'I promise I won't, Gilbert. I'll await your return.' Kissing her quickly, he turned to the door as Gunter knocked. Touching his lips with his fingers, he gave her a special look. How quickly she had become tied to him. It felt as if he had been with her forever. Her heart ached at the thought that she would not see him for a while. She belonged to him; he was her destiny.

As Gilbert and Gunter left for their meeting, Enid knocked at the door. 'I felt that you might be in need of a little company tonight, Gytha. Gunter's already told me, and we were just waiting for Gilbert to tell you. Time will soon pass and you have myself and Godfrey as well,' she said trying to lighten Gytha's mood. Enid realised how much Gytha cared for Gilbert in such a short time. 'Twas only a matter of weeks, and Gytha seemed to have matured into a happy contented married lady, and you could see that both Gilbert and Gytha were madly in love.

The rest of the night until Gilbert's return was spent on days gone by, memories of Gytha's father, Richard, his brother, and her beloved grandfather, George.

Gytha couldn't put in words the fact that she now had an added worry that her beloved Gilbert might not return like her father and uncle didn't. They also touched on Wulf's older brother who had followed her father into battle and not returned either. War left its mark on everyone. It was apparent why everyone wished for peace. Why did people have to fight for things that didn't matter? Only fools would risk their life, but her heart said her Gilbert was not a fool. He was just extremely loyal to his king's cause as her father had been for Harold, and he had not returned. Suddenly it struck her heart what if Gilbert did not return, she would not be able to stand that.

Gilbert arrived at the door just as Enid took her leave to return to her own solar. She had gaged the time right. Gilbert would want to spend some quality time with Gytha before he left tomorrow. She smiled to herself. He would make sure he had memories tonight to carry with him until his return. Enid could not help thinking how romantic it would be for him and Gytha when this new battle would be finished, and he could come back to Alder-Sea. That was all Gytha needed to hang on to.

'Well, Enid, we timed that right,' Gilbert said. 'We will see you in the morning before I leave for the north. You will look after Gytha for me, won't you?' he asked of her.

'She will be my priority, my lord. Gunter's and Godfrey's as well. She will come to no harm in our keeping.'

'Good, that's what I like to hear. Goodnight, Enid,' and with that, he watched Enid enter her solar.

Shutting and putting the bar across the door, he placed the goblet back on the table from where Gytha had taken it. She thought he might like a drink before he retired. Instead, he held her close to his heart. It was as if he wanted to imprint his body with hers before he went. He would not be content until he was back beside her. Inside, he knew for certain that he would be back. She was his destiny. Fate had led him to her, and she had been waiting to be awoken by his love. Gytha was his and his alone, he thought, as he carried her to his bed.

Chapter 19

Morning arrived too soon. Gytha awoke to find that she was being held tightly in Gilbert's arms. She traced her finger down his cheek, and his eyes quickly opened. He rolled her over. He needed that memory of her warm body to take with him. It was sometime later that he rose from the bed.

Making the fire up, he said, 'I will wash first. Wulf will be here soon with bread to break our fast.' He had already hung a can of water for Gytha to wash, but he himself would manage with cold water. Going behind the screen, he poured water into the stone bowl to cleanse himself. As he walked out to dress, Gytha once more was amazed at the beauty of his body. His muscles were taut and lean. For a man so gentle in bed, his body was full of energy and strength, ready to fight.

Soon Wulf was at the door with their breakfast. Gytha had washed in the warm water that Gilbert had put to warm and had put on a cream silk gown that Gilbert liked. She forced herself to smile. It would not be right for him to ride into battle worrying about her happiness. She needed to be positive so that he would concentrate on being safe. Sitting quietly, they enjoyed the fresh fruit and meat that Wulf provided.

Once they finished eating, Gilbert started to place clothing and his personal effects for one of the serfs to collect and pack on his wagon. His broad-sword he cleaned and oiled and hung from his belt. He placed his spare helmet, mail tunic, and spare weapons to be transferred with the rest of the items.

Quickly kissing her, he said, 'I must now go and supervise the transfer of my goods. I will be back, my sweet.'

'I will come with you, Gilbert,' Gytha said looking into his grey eyes, 'Your time too has to fortify me until your return.' Grasping her hand, he led her from the solar along the corridor. Both were silent, occupied by their own thoughts as they strolled through the main hall into the courtyard.

Gilbert kissed her hand and joined Gunter and began to bark out orders. There was a flurry of activity as wagons were packed with essentials and weapons from the stores. Horses were saddled and banners flew in the wind. It took quite a lot of organisation to prepare. The horses pawed the ground with their hooves as if they were impatient to be on their way. Gunter and Gilbert had ordered that a soldier should be posted on guard at all times on the bailey. On the perimeter of the village, there had been extra fences erected to give more protection to the manor. Gilbert and Rolf spoke to Gunter, giving him last minute instructions.

Gilbert walked back to Gytha. Taking her hand and leading her into the doorway to give them more privacy, he held her in his arms slightly away from him.

'I am your husband, Gytha. You do understand that makes you mine.'

'I do, Gilbert.'

'Then you understand that no man must touch you other than me.'

Gytha's face was grave; however, it did not stop her cheek dimpling as she replied with a smile, 'Nor any maid you, my lord, you are my husband.'

Gilbert threw his head back and chuckled, 'I see we will be a match for each other when I get back. Take care, my

sweet, and time will pass quickly. I will be back soon.'
Pulling her into his arms, he held her tightly as he kissed
her once more then led her back to where Godfrey and
Rolf stood.

Gytha could not help holding his hand tightly
whispering, 'Stay safe, my lord, and come back soon.'

Stooping and kissing her quickly again, he turned to
Gunter and Godfrey, 'Take care of her, my good friends.'

Turning, he strode to his destrier and mounted. Rolf
rode at his side to join him in leading the column of
soldiers with him, giving the order to urge them forward.
Watching the soldiers and Gilbert ride away, Gytha
suddenly ran back into the manor making her way with
great speed to the bailey. Taking her handkerchief, she
waved it franticly. Gilbert must have glanced back because
he broke his rank from the lead and rode back to the last
soldiers. Raising his hand, he saluted her, acknowledging
her last goodbye, then turned his horse and rode quickly
back to the front of the column.

Gytha stood there on the bailey until the last bit of dust
had settled. She sat down on the floor, and a stray tear slid
down her cheek. She had been frightened and unsure of
herself when Gilbert had told her he wanted to marry her.
Goodness knows she had not thought of being a married
lady. Now she was, Gytha wished with all her heart that
she could have kept him by her side. Yes, she enjoyed
being cared for and loved by her knight in shining armour.

The trapdoor to the bailey opened, and Enid quietly sat
down beside her. Neither uttered a word. Enid understood
how Gytha felt, and she was glad that Gilbert had changed
his mind and taken Rolf with him. Perhaps soon they
would have an answer from King William allowing Gunter
to marry her. She too would know the heartache that came
with marrying a knight.

Enid at last spoke, 'It won't be long before suppertime, Gytha. You will be required to sit at the head of the table with Gunter and Godfrey.'

'Yes, and of course yourself, Enid. We best go down and show a brave face, and we need to change our clothes.' Enid smiled back at Gytha as she stood and smoothed her gown. Walking to the trapdoor, she was surprised to see Godfrey waiting at the bottom of the steps. Holding his hand out, he helped her from the last step then waited for Enid to alight.

'My Lord Gunter has sent me to tell you to make haste. He will soon be here to escort you to supper, and I will accompany him, my lady,' he said. Gytha could see the concern and sympathy in the look he gave her. Putting a brave smile on her face, she tried hard to appear to be in control. Gytha knew that Godfrey would only worry about her, and she did not wish for him to carry a heavier burden. Godfrey still mourned for his friend, George. Gytha still thought about him but the last few weeks had dimmed the memory of him. He was still her beloved grandfather, but the newness of being a married lady had given her a lot more to think of.

Leaving Gytha and Enid by their solar, he said he would be back quite quickly so don't dawdle because he would not like the remaining soldiers to be kept waiting for their supper. The ones that dined first would then relieve the ones that had been on guard for the most of the day, and they would be dining later than them. He would not like for them to have to wait too long for their supper.

As promised, the two knights came for Gytha and Enid. The two girls had only enough time for a quick wash and to quickly change their gowns before the two men returned.

As they entered the main hall, the Norman soldiers and the Saxons were in a jovial mood; the two races had merged as one. The good-natured banter could be heard against the clatter of wooden trenchers being placed in front of the seated people.

The serfs soon had the top table served with pies, birds and suckling pigs. Everyone seemed to eat with gusto. Enid tried to encourage Gytha to eat a little more as she only picked at the food on her trencher. Gunter insisted to Enid that Gytha would eat when she was hungry. She was missing Gilbert and that was understandable.

After supper, Gytha realised that Enid would want to walk with Gunter around the gardens, so when Enid suggested that she joined her in the solar, Gytha said, 'I need to be by myself for tonight, Enid. You take a walk with Gunter, and you can join me tomorrow when my thoughts are not so sad in Gilbert leaving me.'

'Are you sure, Gytha?'

'Aye, I'm sure, Enid. I just miss him already, and I would not be good company.'

'I will be in to you after I have broken my fast, Gytha. We can walk in the gardens if the weather is clement.'

Gytha gave Enid a smile, and Godfrey said, 'You go for your walk, Enid. I will escort Gytha back to her solar.' For the old knight, things were changing too quickly. He too would miss Gilbert who had been considerate to his needs in the short time he'd been here. He had changed lots of things at Alder-Sea, and his forceful character had brought people into line. He would miss the strength that Gilbert seemed to exude in the running of the manor. Still, he thought Gunter was strong of character too and would know how to follow Gilbert in the running of the village and people. He would have to put his trust in Gunter, but he was sure that he was much like his Lord Gilbert.

'Goodnight, Gytha, time will pass quickly, and my Lord Gilbert will soon be back, my dear.' Opening the door for her, he quickly checked the solar.

'Thank you. So you think that he will be back quickly? I hope so too,' she said with a small smile.

'I do, my lady, so don't be sad. Now make sure you put the bar across the door. We will be watching over you for our Lord Gilbert. I will see you tomorrow,' he said trying to sound positive. The child had suffered too much with this war, but now she appeared to be happy as Gilbert's wife. He hoped she would not have to suffer more loss.

Gytha did as she had been bid, placing the bar that was a little heavy across the doorway. She threw herself on the bed and gave way to the tears that had threatened to erupt all day. She lay there and cried herself to sleep. Why did Gilbert have to go? She realised that she would be lonely without him even though there was a village full of people that loved her.

Waking up cold in the night, she dragged the bearskin over her for warmth and thought about lying in Gilbert's arms. Try as she might, she couldn't find sleep again that night. The faint fingers of dawn crept into the solar through the window slats cut high in the chamber walls.

Dragging herself from the bed, she poured some water to wash, dressed and put logs and kindling wood in the fireplace, and she added some of the rushes that had dried up on the floor. Taking off the bar on the door, she was surprised to see Wulf sitting on a roughly hewn stool outside her solar.

'What are you doing there?' she asked.

'My Lord Gunter instructed me that I am to sleep in the day and stay outside your door at night to ensure you have everything you require, my lady,' he said awkwardly.

'Now, Wulf, since when have I been my lady? We played in the woods as children. I'm still Gytha.'

'I know, but I need to address you correctly. I don't want Lord Godfrey or Lord Gunter to box my ears, do I?' he said with a grin. This brought a smile to her face. Her grandfather had warned more than once that he would, but funnily enough, he never had.

'Well, my good friend, Wulf, you can bring some fresh rushes for the floor and some prepared rush bundles ready for the sconces to light tonight.'

'Of course, Gytha,' he said scurrying off to the far end of the corridor where there were ample rushes in an alcove.

Once he had brought the required rushes for the floor and bundles for the sconces, Gytha said, 'Thank you, Wulf. Now you have done that, alert the kitchen that I am abroad and need to break my fast. Then you, my friend, can retire to your quarters to sleep.'

'I must admit, Gytha, I'm ready to rest.'

'Why my Lord Gunter thinks you need to be at my beck and call, I cannot think. I'm sure our friend Enid will be keeping me company throughout today. It would have been nice for you to join in our speech. Now away to the kitchen, then you can rest.'

'Aye, I will go at once,' he said with a smile turning smartly to go in the direction of the kitchens.

Gytha sighed as she spread sweet-smelling herbs into the fresh rushes on the floor. Her mind was on Gilbert. She had sorely missed her lord's embrace last night. How she wished he had not gone.

When she had been a maid and not a married lady, such thoughts would not have entered her head; however, now he was all she thought of.

There was a gentle knock on the door. 'Enter,' Gytha called, and a young kitchen maid entered with enough food for Enid as well.

'Enid has requested I bring her food in with yours, my lady. She is but a moment behind me.'

'Thank you, Ada. You may put it on the small table there. Are you enjoying your new position in the kitchens?'

'Yes, my lady, I am. Wally is most kind to me.'

'Good,' was all that Gytha said. Her mind was thinking, *that is strange for Wally. He used to work Enid really hard and was always scolding her.*

The next minute, Enid was there at the door as the young kitchen maid left. Enid passed her coming into Gytha's solar.

'How are you this morning, Gytha? Still missing Gilbert, I vow.'

'Yes, 'tis strange that I feel this way. Truth be known, I like being a married lady, and I wish he hadn't gone.'

'Take heart, Gytha, he will soon be back. Time passes quickly, and think what a homecoming you will give him,' Enid said with a smile.

'Aye,' Gytha answered her friend with a slight longing in her voice. 'Now let's eat, then we can walk in the gardens for a while.' Both girls sat down to break bread together.

As Gytha put a morsel of meat in her mouth and swallowed, she suddenly felt sick. Her face turned white. Taking a drink of the fresh water and leaving the ale, she placed her tankard down.

'I must be missing him too much as I feel sickly, perhaps a walk in the gardens will be a good thing for me to sharpen my appetite,' she addressed Enid.

'Yes, you haven't eaten anything, and you are a little pale. The fresh air will do you good,' came Enid's answer.

Clearing the leftover food for the kitchen maid to fetch back, the girls placed a cloak around their shoulders to ensure they were warm enough. Both girls wandered in the rose garden and slowly the sick feeling evaporated, and Gytha began to feel a little better. Her mind was still on Gilbert. Would he need a maid while he was away or would he wait for her as he should? However, he was a man and lots of married men were known to take mistresses as their wives got older. *No*, she thought, *he will only want me, won't he?* her mind questioned.

After picking flowers to take to their solar, they made their way back to quench their thirst. They were just in time to find one of the serfs moving Enid's pallet into Gytha's solar. It made sense for the girls to share, and Gunter to move into Enid's solar for him to be closer for protection if it was needed.

Gunter would not let anything happen to Gilbert's wife or his intended. He was now aware of the tunnel, and if there were any more attacks, it would be his job to hide the girls safely as Godfrey and Gilbert had. Lord George had been very innovative to build this safe escape route to protect himself and his family.

Sitting down and partaking some of the fruit that had been provided with the drink, Gytha immediately felt sick again. It must be because she was upset that Gilbert had left. Her stomach would settle down, she thought.

Just drinking a little more water, she said, 'I think I will rest a little, Enid. If you would like to seek Gunter out, today would be a good time as there will be the complaints to be heard tomorrow, and Gunter expects myself and Godfrey to be present. Besides, I didn't sleep well.'

'If you're sure, Gytha. I will be back quickly in good time for supper?'

'I'm sure, Enid, now go and spend some time with your intended.'

Enid smiled at Gytha, 'You are such a good friend, Gytha.'

As Enid left, Gytha went and sat before the fire. For some reason, she once more felt sick and didn't dare lie down yet. She would soon get used to Gilbert being away, and she would feel more like herself.

Getting up and splashing some cold water upon her face and hair, it refreshed her a little. Then moving away from the fire, the sickness that had overcome her began to recede. Getting up, she decided to lie down after all. She would then soon feel better.

Sometime later, Enid returned. Gently shaking Gytha, she said, 'It's time to get ready for supper, Gytha. Do you feel better for your rest?'

'Aye, Enid, I do.'

'Well, I'll pour you a small goblet of wine, then we can ready for Gunter and Godfrey to escort us to supper.'

'Well, my friend, did you enjoy your time with Gunter?' Enid's face coloured up.

'I did, Gytha. I hope William soon sends word that we may be betrothed. I can't wait to be a married lady too.'

Chapter 20

Over the next few weeks, Gytha's sick feeling continued, and she was now physically sick, especially in the morning. Enid had suggested that Edgar could give her a potion. It wasn't normal to be sick. Gytha insisted that she would be fine and said no, it was missing Gilbert that was the problem, and it would pass. Enid was dallying with Gunter while Gytha was resting once more, and she mentioned Gytha not feeling well.

'In what way, Enid?' he asked.

'She is always feeling sick, has been sick on a number of occasions, and she is off her food. I suggested she tell Edgar, but she says no.'

'Well, I won't suggest she needs to see Edgar. I have been charged with looking after her by Gilbert, so I will speak to Edgar this very minute, and I have a rough idea of what might be ailing her.'

'What?' asked Enid.

'We will leave the diagnosis to Edgar. I'm sure she will be pleased, my sweet. Now we will go to Edgar immediately. The sooner this is sorted, the less worried you will be.' Both Gunter and Enid made their way to Edgar, who once they had made him aware that Gytha was not well, he smiled.

'Well, let's away and examine my Lady Gytha, then we all will be relieved to know it is something that is quite simple to deal with.'

'Edgar, I will leave it to Enid and yourself, and I will be back as the king has sent me a message that I need to read. The soldier has to ride straight back on William's instructions. I won't be long and I will come back to find out what Gytha's malady is.' Giving a hopeful smile and a slight bow to Enid, he made his way to the soldier that he had left eating in the guardroom.

He had left him there as he went to tell Enid that William's message had arrived. Because Enid was worried about Lady Gytha, he had thought to have Edgar to examine her directly would be prudent. Hopefully, the soldier's news would be good and he came with the answer what they had hoped for. He thought that Gytha's sickness could be one of two things, and they could send news to Gilbert via another way. He would send one of their soldiers if necessary. Making his way to the guardhouse, he found the soldier Henrick Pickadee ready to take to horse.

'I must leave now, my lord. I have another message to deliver, and I have lingered too long and need to be on my way. I hope the news I have delivered is to your liking, my lord,' and with a small bow, he passed the rolled parchment carrying the king's seal to Gunter, then quickly mounted his destrier and rode away at great speed. Gunter made his way to the main hall to read his message.

Gilbert must have spoken highly of him as the king had granted his permission to marry Enid and pointed out that Gilbert was his overlord at the moment and that he could have given that permission himself. However, he was now aware of Gunter's and also of Rolf's loyalty and brave deeds and as soon as he was able to, he would be also granting him deeds to a manor and lands.

Edgar and Enid had arrived at Gytha's solar. She was surprised to see the kindly physician at the door.

'Come in, Edgar, it is kind that you are visiting me,' Gytha said giving Enid a look that said you shouldn't have wasted his time.

'I have been told you are a little sickly, my lady, and I would be failing in my duty if I did not examine you to see what is bothering you.'

''Tis nought, Edgar, I think I must be missing Gilbert more than I thought, and my appetite has not been great.'

'I am the person to decide that, my lady. Lie on the bed,' he instructed.

Gytha looked at him with alarm, 'I'm sure I will be okay, Edgar.'

'Well, there's no harm in making sure, now is there.' She knew it was no good arguing with the good man, so she lay down as she had been instructed. Edgar then asked her a few questions, and she answered to the best of her ability. He then examined her stomach.

'Well, Gytha, there is nothing wrong with you that will hurt you.'

'There isn't, Edgar?'

'No, nothing that will hurt you. Tell me, Gytha, you are aware that when you marry and lie with a man that you could have children?'

Gytha stared and answered, 'Yes, I do.'

'Well, that is all that is wrong. You are having a baby, my lady.'

'A baby,' she repeated, 'Gilbert's baby. Will he be pleased, Edgar?'

'I think he will be more than pleased. I will mix you a potion to help you with the sickness and that bit will soon pass, and I will make sure that you are pampered and indulged until the child puts in an appearance.'

Enid smiled. 'I'm sure that Gilbert will be as proud as a peacock. I can't wait to tell Gunter. He can send a message back to Gilbert if he hasn't left yet.'

'Yes, if you do that, you can come to me to pick up the potion for my Lady Enid. The sickness will abate but a little help managing it will help.'

Both Enid and Edgar left to find Gunter waiting in the great hall.

When Enid imparted the news of Gytha becoming a mother, he replied, 'You wait until Gilbert knows. He will be so proud.'

'You could send news with the young soldier to Gilbert.'

'Alas, my sweet, he had to leave. He has another message to deliver, and he was instructed to make his way straight back.'

'Why didn't you ask him to wait a little longer?' Enid scolded.

Before Gunter could answer, Edgar said, 'I must away and make the potion for my lady. You will remember to call and pick it up, Enid?'

'I will, Edgar,' Enid answered, turning her attention to Gunter as Edgar hurried away. Spying the paper in Gunter's hand, she was taken aback by him pulling her to him.

In an excited embrace, kissing her, he said, 'Lord William has said yes, my love. We can get Father Bernard to hear our betrothal vows and marry within the next few weeks. Are you not happy, my sweet?'

'We can?' she breathed her own excitement at the news from William preceding Gytha being with child. 'I must tell Gytha. She will be so pleased for us, Gunter.'

'As Gilbert will already be. He will be privy to William's decision already. Go and tell Gytha, it might take her mind off feeling sick.'

Scurrying back to Gytha in the solar, she said, 'I must collect your potion from Edgar, but I just had to come and tell you that William says yes, Gunter and I are to be married soon, Gytha.'

Gytha immediately stood and embraced Enid, 'I'm so happy for you, Enid. May the Holy Mother bless you with a baby as quick as she has me. 'Twas the last thought in my head. I do declare, my Lord Gilbert has certainly left me with something to take my mind off him,' she said with a stab at humour.

'I won't be long, Gytha. If I don't go now, Edgar will probably scold me.'

'Well, hurry back and we can decide what you are to wear for your wedding day.' Enid mouthed thank you as she hurried from the solar on her errand to Edgar.

Enid was so excited. She had the pink dress in mind, the one she had worn to wait upon Gytha at her wedding day. It was the best she had. Rushing back to the solar, she saw that Gytha had lain out a cream dress that would hug her under the breast and was edged with blue artificial roses. The sleeves draped down the arm and fell into an elegant point. Enid had not seen it before.

'Do you like it, Enid?'

'I do like it, Gytha.'

'Then it is my and Gilbert's wedding present to you.'

'I don't know what to say, Gytha.'

'Well, don't say anything. Besides, I've never worn it so no one has seen it, and if I know Gunter, he won't want to leave here to buy new presents for you. He takes looking after Alder-Sea for Gilbert seriously. So, your dress is sorted.'

Enid hugged Gytha. 'You are such a good friend, Gytha, and I love you dearly.'

'I too love your companionship and friendship, Enid. We have come such a long way since we were children.'

'Yes, we have,' Enid agreed with a smile. She was certain Gunter would have everything else arranged soon.

The rest of the week passed quickly. Gytha sat in when Gunter and Godfrey were to make any decisions and Father Bernard had been to listen to Gunter and Enid's betrothal vows. Their wedding was to be held in three weeks. It was quick just like when she and Gilbert were wed. She herself had taken to being married very quickly, and she hoped that Enid would be just as pleased with marriage as she had been. In fact, she still longed for Gilbert, and he was never far from her mind.

Three weeks soon passed, and Enid's wedding day was upon them. Gytha was to attend her, and Enid had asked for Wulf to be in attendance. At the moment, Gunter would deny her nothing. They would soon lie together, and he had waited so long, in his mind, whatever Enid wanted, Enid could have.

He was pleased when he asked Enid about a dress for the wedding, and she said she had been given one as a wedding present by Gytha and Gilbert. He already had his grandmother's ring to give her, and everything else would take care of itself. There would be time to treat Enid when Gilbert was back.

Enid dressed in the cream dress that Gytha had given to her, and the seamstress had made her a coronate of forget-me-nots along with a small posy to carry. The pews in the church had also been decorated in cream and blue flowers.

Gunter had a blue uniform made for Wulf to wear for the marriage to make it a special day. Enid walked out of the small church a married lady and from today, she would be known as Lady Enid. She was now married to a knight and had been elevated.

The merrymaking went on into the night. Gunter moved Enid into the solar next to Gytha, so they would both be close to her now to make sure that they were there to keep her safe. Gytha sat late into the night. The merrymaking was an outlet to try and put her longing for Gilbert from her mind, but if anything, it made her long for him more as she remembered her wedding night. When at last she decided to retire, Godfrey escorted her to her solar.

Sensing that Gytha was once again melancholy, he said, 'Time will soon pass, Gytha. Think how exciting it will be when Gilbert is to see his child for the first time when he returns home.'

'Aye, you're right, Godfrey. It will be a great moment in my and Gilbert's life.'

'Goodnight, Gytha,' he bid her.

The next day, Gytha had been up but a short time when Enid knocked quietly on her door. Gunter had gone to check the perimeters of the manor grounds as the soldiers changed watch. The night had been quiet with no incidents to report, and he hoped that would be the last he would see of any renegade soldiers within their forest. Later today, he would take a group of soldiers to do a little more hunting to add to their supplies. He did not want to let the reserves to get too low.

The first thing that Gytha asked, 'Well, did you enjoy becoming a married lady?'

Enid went red, ''Twas not bad, Gytha, and as he said, it got better. I do love him, Gytha. He's my knight in shining armour, and I'm sure you will be happy once Gilbert comes back.'

'Aye, I will be, Enid. It's getting a little better. I just need to hold onto the thought that he will be back soon.'

'After last night, I wouldn't be surprised that I will be with child soon,' Enid said, 'then we could be bringing a family up side by side.'

Gytha smiled and with an attempt at humour, 'Well, we have always done things at the same time, why not this, my friend? I have perceived maidens that are with child, and although their faces bloom, their bodies look cumbersome. Though I long for Gilbert to be back, I hope to give birth before he returns home.'

'I'm sure he will love you whatever you look like, Gytha.'

'We'll see,' came Gytha's answer.

'Now, would you like to walk in the garden? They say that exercise is good for ladies with child.'

'Exercise is what got us with child. I think a walk will be enjoyable,' came Gytha's answer.

'You only need a light cloak, Gytha. I will just get my own from my solar,' Enid said as she slipped away to the solar. Gytha was waiting outside in the corridor when Enid emerged from the solar.

Both girls linked arms and made their way out into the sunshine. As they passed out to the gardens, they watched the Norman soldiers practicing with their broadswords and bows. They needed to keep up their fighting skills even if they weren't needed. Gytha wished for peace. If she was to raise a child, she wanted to do it with Gilbert beside her.

The day passed pleasantly and it soon would-be suppertime. She had decided that she must start a sampler for the child. Her mother had done one when she was born. She would try her needle skills to keep her occupied. She was sure Gunter would want Enid to spend a little more time by his side.

Gytha looked up the sampler her mother had made so that she could see what it was meant to look like. As she examined it, she was sad that she could not remember her mother. It would have been nice to know what she had been like.

The weeks passed quietly, and suddenly six months had passed. Gytha was confined to the solar as her lying in was nearing. She now had a young girl who slept on a pallet in her solar so that there was someone present at all times.

Enid spent most of her spare time at Gytha's side. She too was with child, and both girls stitched small garments under the supervision of the seamstress. Gytha was quite pleased with her work. She had also nearly finished the sampler. She had left space for the birth date and the name of the child.

Gytha had also made a few improvements in the solar, and Godfrey in his spare time had made two cribs, one for Gytha's child and one for Enid's.

Godfrey had settled down and had stopped grieving for George. He knew he would meet him again in the hereafter and that had given him peace of mind. He watched over Gytha like she was his own daughter. He would lay down his own life to keep her safe for Gilbert who by now he admired immensely. Winter was once more upon them, and the wind outside was cutting with snow on the ground. She had no word from Gilbert and prayed nightly that he was safe. The cold weather outside restricted the exercise of walking out in the gardens.

Gytha was still restless so Enid and she would walk in the manor throughout the main rooms even though she was supposed to stay in the solar. They would look to see that the work she had requested had been completed. They had started to have furniture made to grace some of the empty solars. It was of no use them being there without them being habitable. She and Enid put their heads together and soon each solar contained the basics required to be of use. Gytha had instructed that a larger screen be made to divide the washing facilities better.

Room for the crib had been made and the woodcutter in the village had made a chest for the new child's clothing, and a larger rail had been fashioned to hang Gilbert's threads as well as hers. Also, she had commissioned a carved chair in matching oak for Gilbert. She herself had stitched cushions for comfort, and she hoped that he would like it.

It was February, and Gytha awoke in pain. Anna, the young maid that slept in her solar, was soon knocking on Enid's door to alert her. Both her and Gunter dressed in a hurry. Gunter went at once to alert Edgar, and Enid went straight to her friend's side, sending the young maid to have water heated and extra linen brought into the solar.

It was a long night as Enid rung out cloths to cool Gytha's head. Edgar and the seamstress worked hard to help Gytha throughout the night when suddenly Edgar said, 'It's a boy, a son for Lord Gilbert.'

Passing the child to Enid, he beckoned the seamstress back behind the screen, as a second head began to crown. Enid had washed the child and wrapped it in a clean length of linen, lying the small, scrunched bundle of humanity in the crib.

Suddenly, another cry rent the air as the seamstress slapped the child on the back. She passed another child into the arms of Enid to wash and wrap a daughter also for Lord Gilbert.

'No more, please,' Enid said in amazement. After seeing Gytha struggle all night to give birth, she wasn't looking forward to her birthing day.

Once the seamstress had cleaned Gytha up and put fresh linen on the bed, they made a warm bowl of gruel for her. She had been told not to drink ale or wine whilst feeding the child, although a wet nurse would be sent from the village to help in the night.

When she was feeling more rested, Enid placed the boy in Gytha's arms, 'Pray, what sex is it, Enid?'

'Why, a healthy boy, Gytha,' she said, and she walked back around the screen. Somehow, Enid realised, Gytha had missed the fact that she had given birth to a boy and a girl.

Walking back in with the other bundle, she asked, 'Have you room for this other bundle in your arms, Gytha, your and Gilbert's daughter?' Gytha was astounded. Two children?!

'Both at the same time, Enid?' said Gytha in amazement as she gazed down at her babies with wonder.

'Yes, Gytha, only you could manage that. You are the best at everything,' Enid replied laughing at her friend's expression.

'Tush! I declare that my Lord Gilbert has left me with plenty to do whilst he is away fighting for William.'

'They are beautiful, Gytha. Gilbert will be so proud of you.' At this point, there was a scratching at the door. Enid went to the door to see both Gunter and Godfrey waiting to enter. Both men were astounded that she had given birth safely, and to two babies at once.

Godfrey said in awe, 'Can we hold them, Gytha?'

'Yes, you can have the boy and Gunter the girl, and that means that you will both have to help with them until Gilbert returns.'

They both answered in unison, 'It will be a pleasure. We will be their father until Gilbert returns.'

Over the next few weeks, Gytha and the wet nurse managed to feed the babies between them. The boy she had named William Richard George Bayeux, William for the king to please Gilbert, Richard after her father, and George for her grandfather. The girl was to be Anna Elise

217

Rose. She had to name them herself because Gilbert wasn't here, and she needed to church them.

Gytha could not wait for Gilbert to come back. They could have sent a soldier to take the news, but they might not find which area he was in, and she decided no, he might have his mind on them instead of himself. Gytha needed him to come back. She would not want them to grow up without a father.

It was just seven weeks later that Enid gave birth to her little girl, Camile. Gytha assisted at the birth leaving a wet nurse and the young girl that had not left her side since she had joined her in her solar to help. Now, she was their nurse. The twins were almost two months old and were thriving and putting on weight. The boy had his father's grey eyes, whilst the girl had Gytha's lavender blue eyes. They were happy and content babies, and Gytha thought that they seemed to recognise her.

Both Enid and Gytha spent most of the day together with their babies. It was now the beginning of April, and the weather was more clement. Occasionally, they would leave the three children with the nurse to look after while they took a walk. Sometimes, the three of them could be seen walking in the gardens, each holding a well-wrapped up child, for them to take some fresh air.

It was on such a day that a young soldier rode into the courtyard of the manor. He slid from his horse at the side of Godfrey who had been standing waiting for Gytha and Enid who were making their way back from the rose garden.

'A message from Lord Gilbert, sir. He is but two days away and wishes you to know he will soon be here.'

'You look weary. You must go inside and refresh yourself,' Godfrey said as he recognised the young soldier to be Henrick Pickadee. Leaving the soldier to enter the manor, he strode towards the three girls emerging from the rose garden.

'Good news, Gytha. Gilbert is on his way back and is just two days away.' Gytha's free hand went to her mouth.

'Thanks to the Holy Mother he is safe.' Godfrey quickly relieved Gytha of the child she was carrying in her arms. He did not want her to drop the child in her excitement.

Gunter had ridden off that morning to pick up much needed spices and stores that they did not have here at Castle Alder-sea and would not be back for three days, as Gytha and Enid had added a list of much needed threads and fripperies. They hoped he would be back sooner. Gunter would be really pleased to see Gilbert and Rolf. Both girls were over the moon. Enid because that sad look that she perceived in Gytha's eyes would disappear once he was back in her bed.

Gytha at once looked at Enid, 'I must order a bath to be brought for the morning. I must be at my best for Gilbert's return.' She hugged Enid in excitement. Gilbert was coming home, how wonderful! Her heart was singing with excitement.

Hurrying back to the solar, she began to look through her threads to see what gown to wear tomorrow just in case he arrived at suppertime. The kitchens needed to be told they must have their finest fare ready for Gilbert's return. As she viewed her rail holding her gowns, she came to the blue silk. Almost at once, she gazed upon her wedding gown, the cream fine linen with small pink artificial roses sewn around the hem and neck. She wore this dress when she went to him as a maid. Her mind was made up that she would wear this dress to remind him of their betrothal.

It had been a magical night. Gilbert was still the knight that had rescued her from the dragon. She hoped he would understand how much she had missed him, and she fully planned to show him.

Quickly taking up the rushes off the floor and feeding them to the fire, she swept the floor just as she had in the past as Guy. Once this was done, she distributed the fresh ones down. Looking in the babies' cribs, she emptied the soft straw from each one and replaced with fresh at the same time ensuring there was no hard pieces. Then she took several pieces of clean linen and covered the straw.

She would bathe the babies and make sure their threads were kept clean in readiness for them to meet their father. He had no knowledge of them. Gytha wanted them to smell sweet and clean for this very important meeting. Would he fall in love with them as she had the moment she had set eyes on their small faces?

Anna and the wet nurse would soon be back with them. They had taken them outside in the spring sunshine for some fresh air. Picking up a cloth, she made sure that all the surfaces were clean. She must admit that if she had attended to these chores herself more, the wet nurse and Girta would have a little more rest.

All at once, she felt quite restless. She was impatient for the next two days to pass. Having waited so patiently for the last months, she was finding it impossible to wait any longer. Gytha had never felt this way and knew she would not sleep this night. To be held in Gilbert's strong arms was all that had kept her sane through the long nights of months past.

Enid came back to the solar. Going into Gytha's, she smelt the sweet smell of herbs amongst the rushes.

'It smells really good in here, and it's not rose water that I can smell. I will have to spread some herbs amongst the rushes on our solar floor for when Gunter returns from fetching supplies.'

Gytha smiled, 'What are you trying to say, Enid?'

'That perhaps Lord Gilbert won't be interested in the housekeeping chores that you have completed when he sets eyes on you.'

Gytha proceeded to say that she would take turns in watching from the bailey and as soon as she saw any dust clouds on the road, she would come down and dress, ready to be at the manor door to offer Gilbert the welcome cup, something that they had not offered him the first day that he had rode up to the manor. This time it would be so different. He would realise how many people cared for and loved him, a welcome to make him glad to be home. Thinking of her grandfather, she hoped he was happy for her and that he realised how happy Gilbert had made her.

Girta had laid the twins on the large bed. She would bathe the children, and they would be fed before they were laid in their crib to rest.

'Now, Gytha, I will go and see to little Lord Hinds and then ready myself for supper. My Lord Godfrey will have to escort both of us to the main hall.'

'I feel that my stomach won't allow me to eat too much, I'm so excited,' Gytha declared.

Suppertime was much as usual the Normans and Saxons alike imbibed a large quantity of beer. Everyone was more jovial than normal knowing that Lord Gilbert returning made them sure that some of them wouldn't be called back to take up arms at William's side. They would be able to stay here at the manor. Fighting was hopefully a thing of the past. After over a year here, they were happy to have such an easy job of defending the manor.

Gilbert, when he had been here and watching his men break bread together, would know of any undercurrents or grievances running through the ranks and would be able to defuse them before they exploded. He was a people person and had great people management skills, although Gunter had kept everything running smoothly in Gilbert's absence.

Godfrey said, 'I've time to help watch on the bailey, my lady, if you will allow me to help, and I too will come and warn you of Lord Gilbert's arrival. That will make four of us. We can take a slice each to ensure we are ready to welcome him back.'

'I would appreciate that, Godfrey, and of course, the lookout will be up there too, but he has to complete his full guard before he comes down.'

'I know but it will make it easier if we all do our bit and of course, you need to look your best.'

'Thank you, Godfrey.'

'Don't thank me, Gytha. I'm here to watch over you not only for Gilbert but for my old friend George. Like Enid and yourself, we were friends as small children the bond went deep. I'm convinced George and I will meet again on another plane.' Gytha smiled. Her fondness for Godfrey also went deep. She hoped he would be here with Gilbert and herself for years to come. It would be nice for William and Anna to have him as a protector as they grew over their informative years. He would be a great source of education for her children in years to come. *Besides*, she thought, *I am selfish. I need some familiar faces with me as well as new faces.*

Chapter 21

Morning came, and Gytha rose and put on a loose robe. She had asked for a bath to be brought to her at first light. The serfs arrived with large cans of hot water, and she had cold water in a container to cool it if necessary. Girta was already attending to the children, and Gytha had added to the water a concoction of oil perfumed with spring flowers and had a fresh bar of perfumed soap. She took time to ensure that she scrubbed her skin clean. Once dried, she applied rose water liberally. She wanted to be at her best when Gilbert arrived home.

Sitting and feeding the twins with the help of her wet nurse, they were soon contented and back in their cribs. Eating very little off the trencher that the kitchen maid had provided, she was too excited to settle. She took a cloak to ward off the morning chill and bid Girta to stay with the children while she made her way to the bailey. Gytha intended to watch for an hour.

When she appeared through aperture of the trapdoor, it was to find that Godfrey was already watching for approaching travellers in the distance. Godfrey smiled at Gytha's enthusiasm for her Lord Gilbert to arrive home. He too remembered the feeling of young love when he was first married. His mind rested on the only woman he had loved. He knew soon after she died that he would never be able to replace her. With a sigh, Godfrey turned his attention to Gytha.

'I will watch, Gytha. If I need to leave the bailey, I will let you know, and then you can take my place.'

'I'm restless, Godfrey. I will keep you company for a while. You don't mind?'

'No, I don't mind. I will enjoy your company; however, the wind blows cold up here so you must not stay here too long. Besides your children will need you also, agreed?'

'Yes,' came her short answer as she leant on the brickwork of the bailey wall, her eyes glued to the horizon.

After an hour watching, Godfrey said, 'Why don't you go and see that the children are alright? I'm parched, and you could send a serf with some ale and bread for myself and yon soldier who was here before me. I'm sure he would appreciate the kindness.' Gytha reluctantly left the place where she had been leaning.

'I will, my Lord Godfrey. I will get someone to bring a stool and cushion. I'm sure you will benefit from sitting. You will still be able to see if you rest on a stool.' Godfrey smiled thinking was it so obvious that he was ageing, it was something that no one could change. Turning his attention back to watching the skyline, he began his long vigil again.

It was but a short time later that two serfs arrived on the bailey, one carrying a jug of ale and meat and bread, and the second was carrying a stool for the elderly knight and a cushion for him to sit on.

He decided that yes, he would sit for a while and then let the soldier rest his legs. His time watching as a lookout would be much longer than Godfrey being there. Not a lot happened until just before suppertime when the not too chatty guard suddenly alerted Godfrey.

'Look to the right, my lord, there is a small party approaching.'

'Thank you. I will alert my Lady Gytha. Keep watching because we cannot be sure if it's our Lord Gilbert.' Quickly making his way through the trapdoor, he made his way to Gytha's solar.

'Gytha, there is a party approaching the manor. We will make sure who it is, so if you wish to come to the entrance door in case it is Lord Gilbert, you have time to ready yourself.' With that, Godfrey walked quickly back to the main hall making his way to the manor entrance.

Gytha quickly made her way to the screen to change her gown. Picking her wedding gown from the rail she dressed herself.

'Girta, you must stay in here with the children, and I will go to greet whoever our visitors are. I must get the serf to fetch the welcome cup in readiness for whomever it may be.' Her heart was beating hard against her chest as she was hoping that it would be Gilbert. How happy she would be if it was. Stopping at the kitchen on her way out, she ordered them to bring her the welcome cup. Hurrying to the entrance, she was soon waiting in the doorway to greet whoever it was.

It wasn't long before a group of soldiers swept into the courtyard with a couple of waggons. Gytha's eyes searched the party for Gilbert, but he was nowhere to be seen. Just as she was about to ask, a soldier slid off his horse and helped a young maiden to alight from the wagon. She was tall with straight blond hair down to her waist. Gytha's hand's went automatically to her growing blond curls. It was now shoulder length. This reminded her of someone, but she couldn't quite make out who. Standing holding the welcome cup, she waited for the maid to announce who she was.

Even before she said, 'Welcome to our manor,' the girl addressed Gytha.

'You there, take me to your Lord Gilbert's solar. That will be the best, and I will sup in there. He would want me to await him there.' Gytha clutched the front of her dress, spilling the wine in the goblet.

She spoke up clearly. 'I'm afraid Lord Gilbert's solar is occupied. I'm sure Lord Gilbert will be happy for you to reside in any of the unoccupied solars. Is Lord Gilbert aware of your visit?'

'Will you risk Gilbert's displeasure when he knows that a Saxon maid has denied me the best solar in the manor?' she asked. Gytha stretched herself to her full height as Godfrey went to interrupt her speech.

'Let me be the judge of that. Wulf, escort this lady to the solar that is underneath the bailey that has just been furnished. It is quite comfortable. After all, it has just been made ready for visitors. Then away to the kitchen to arrange food for our visitor.'

Gytha was white with anger. If Gilbert had brought a cuckhold into their manor, he was mistaken if he thought she would stand by and let it just go over her head. She waited for a whole year for him to return home, and he had sent a mistress to grace his solar. Turning, she rushed back to her solar thinking only of her children, anger showing in every move she made.

Enid followed her, worried about what her friend was about to do. Surely, he would not be so crass as to do as they all thought. The lady had not thought it necessary to announce herself and placed herself in Gilbert's bed. Most men who took a mistress would have kept them hidden but not this one. Was it a Norman custom? If it was, it wasn't a very clever one.

Knocking and entering Gytha's solar, Enid found Gytha marching up and down.

'How dare he bring that woman here!' she raved in anger, her small fists clenched.

'It might not be what we think, Gytha,' Enid tried to counsel.'

'I'm not stupid. What else could it be? She was so sure of herself, as if she was his wife.'

'Gytha, don't upset yourself so. You will make yourself ill. Wait until my Lord Gilbert arrives back. It might not be as it seems.'

'I swear he will pay for this if he tries to lie about it. I trusted him. How could he?' Holding her face in her hands, Gytha gave way to the tears that she had held back successfully as she had drawn on her strength to face the maiden that Gilbert had sent ahead. He who stated he spoke the truth, *what sort of truth?* she questioned in her mind.

'Come dry your eyes, Gytha. You need to draw on the strength that the Holy Mother has supplied you with. Supper will be soon, and we need to show a good face in front of the rest of the occupiers in the manor, and I'm sure it would be best not to upset my Lord Godfrey. He loves you as a daughter.'

'Aye,' Gytha said, trying to hold the tears back. 'I would not wish him to see me upset.'

Going behind the screen, she ripped her betrothal dress from top to bottom. Pouring water, she washed and dried her face, purposely choosing a dress that Gilbert had not supplied, kicking her wedding dress into the far corner. She went and quietly and sat by the fire after first gazing at her sleeping children.

'Gytha, please stay here while I ready myself for supper. We only have each other until Gunter returns. Perhaps he will be back before Gilbert even and will have some thought on the matter.'

'You go, Enid, I won't leave here until you come back. I have Girta.' She had suddenly remembered the children's nurse sitting quietly by the cribs. What must she think? She had been raving like a fish wife; hopefully, Girta would hold her tongue and not repeat what she had seen in the solar.

When Enid returned, Gytha had summoned up all her strength to smile and control how she felt. She was aware that if Gilbert had sent this woman, this mistress, that there was nothing else here for her at Alder-Sea. But what of her children? She couldn't bear to leave them, and what could she offer them if she tried to take them with her? They were her babies. Hers, not that woman's. There was no way that she would let her near them.

It wasn't long before Godfrey arrived at the solar. The first thing that he said was, 'Are you more settled, my lady?'

'No more than I was earlier, Godfrey. I am no fool. My Lord Gilbert owes me an explanation which I await with interest.'

'Don't torture yourself, my lady. There could be a simple explanation.'

'I think the fact that she appeared to think that she was to sleep in Gilbert's solar speaks for itself, Godfrey.'

'Godfrey, this cannot be right. Don't judge him until he is here and explains his actions,' came Enid's voice. She had never seen her friend so angry. She hoped that the maid did not decide to join them for supper, for she could not see Gytha holding her tongue if the maid looked down on her again. The stranger's slight against Saxons had not gone unnoticed.

Godfrey stepped back allowing Gytha and Enid to proceed him. Both were quiet. Godfrey prayed to the Holy Mother in his mind that they were wrong, for his loyalty would be for his friend's granddaughter and not for Gilbert whilst Enid was sick in her stomach for what her friend might have to endure.

Suppertime came to an end and true to her word, the maid never showed her face and did stay in the solar. At least Gytha did not have to see her again before Gilbert arrived. They could explain themselves together. Godfrey stood and held Gytha's hands.

'Gytha, try not to fret and try to have a good night's rest, for whatever has led the maid has been upsetting for you and could become distressing for Gilbert. Try not to give yourself answers for now.'

'That, Godfrey, is easier said than done; however, nothing can be achieved until Gilbert does me the courtesy of explaining himself. Goodnight, Godfrey. Goodnight, Enid.' Giving a sad smile, Gytha entered her solar and quietly closed the door.

The children were already fast asleep, and the nurse was sleeping on her pallet. Gytha sat on the chair by the fire. Sleep would elude her, so she sat looking into the flames of the fire.

She woke much later cold and aching. She had fallen asleep where she sat. Throwing a couple of logs on the fire, she wearily lay down on the bed. She forced herself to rest as she would have to feed the twins with the wet nurse. It was a weary Gytha that rose to help see to the twins.

Her food was delivered from the kitchen. Taking a drink, she tried to eat a little bread, but it stuck in her throat. She dressed herself in a dress that Grandfather had purchased for her.

She decided to take some time up by visiting Enid in her solar. She would not do Gilbert the honour of greeting him with the welcome cup. Besides, he might come straight to the solar thinking that his new lady would be waiting for him. She had been so sure that he was trustworthy. How had she misjudged him so.

Knocking at Enid's solar, the door was opened, and she said, 'I need the comfort of you by my side, Enid.'

'Are you not going to the entrance for Gilbert's return?'

'No, my friend, he won't be interested in me waiting for him. Let us see whom he seeks out, shall we?' Enid knew this would not go down well with Lord Gilbert especially because he had been absent for over a year. Holding her tongue, she drew Gytha into her solar and towards the two chairs by the fire. It wasn't long before they heard Wulf banging on the door of the solar and the nurse scolding him for awakening the babies.

Enid opened the door. 'What is it, Wulf?'

'It's our Lord Gilbert. He's just rode into the courtyard. I thought my Lady Gytha would want to know.' Gytha joined Enid in the passageway and gave way to her feelings.

'If Gilbert Bayeux wants to see me, he must seek me out,' she spit out in anger. All her intentions left her, and her face already red with anger.

At that moment, Gilbert came into view striding up the corridor. 'I thought you were ill, my love. I expected you to meet me. Have you not missed me?' he asked with a puzzled look on his face.

Without a minute to spare, she launched herself at him. 'You thought I would greet you when you have sent a maid on before you to share your solar, your cuckold? You misjudge me, my lord.'

'Stop it, you will hurt yourself,' he spit out holding her hands behind her and gripping her body close as she made to strike out at him. Gytha kicked out and made contact with his shin.

'That hurt, you little shrew! I know naught of any maid. Now be quiet, or I'll be forced to show you who is master here. How have you become such a sharp scold full hussy in the time I have been away?'

'You dare accuse me?' she spat still trying to struggle to release her hands.

At that moment, there were footsteps approaching them. Gytha looked to see who it was, someone else to listen in to her heartache. It was Rolf holding the maid in question firmly by the hand.

Gilbert loosened his hold as he said, 'Marianne, what are you doing here?' Gytha saw her moment and kicked him hard once more on the shin.

Quickly holding her hands tight again, he said, 'What on earth has got into you?'

'You ask, my lord, when you send this wench to share your chamber?'

The maid began to laugh. 'I thought your solar would be the best in the castle, Gilbert, but yon Saxon maid firmly told me that it was already occupied.'

'This Saxon maid is Lady Gytha Bayeux, my wife, Marianne, and whilst in our home you will show some respect. We are no longer children trying to score points off each other.'

'Well, if Lady Gytha had told me whom she was, I would have understood,' Marianne answered.

'Like you told me who you were and still have not told me?'

Gilbert turned to his wife smiling. 'You were jealous, my sweet,' once more relaxing his hold. And once more, Gytha aimed another kick.

'Who is she?' Gytha demanded.

'My sister. I swear I did not know she was here. She is always trying to get the better of me, and this time you have not let her.'

'Your sister, why did she not say?'

'She has always been bossy.'

'Well, Marianne, this is one place that you might not get your own way.'

Smiling back at Gytha she declared, 'I don't mind that. I'm back with Rolf, and William has given him permission to wed me. I'm sorry, Gytha, can we start again?'

'I'm sorry too. I should not have accused before speaking to Gilbert, but you were a little bossy,' she said with a smile.

Suddenly, Gilbert and Gytha's solar door opened and shrieks and wails of the babies rent the air.

'My lady, I can't quiet them, they are hungry,' the young Girta advised her. Gytha lifted her skirt and quickly made her way into the solar. Gilbert followed wondering who was making the horrendous noise. Walking in behind her, he looked at the little bundle in her arms.

'Who...?' he said not finishing his sentence. As he remembered Marianne saying that Gytha had informed her that his solar was occupied but not by who, he had thought it was just Gytha.

'Gilbert,' she said, her cheeks dimpling as she smiled, 'Let me introduce you to Lord William Richard George Bayeux.' Gilbert took the child off her looking at the small face as the grey eyes of the child studied his face. Gytha gave a little cough, 'And this, my lord, is your daughter, Lady Anna Elise Rose Bayeux.' This was almost too much for Gilbert.

'Two at once?' Both children had their mother's blond curls.

'Yes, Gilbert, you left me with quite a present, and I love them both so much.'

'And me, Gytha?' he asked his eyes searching hers. '

'Yes,' was all she could utter as her eyes never left his face.

'Perhaps you will show me later, my sweet,' he whispered to her. Marianne walked over and took one of the babies, and Rolf took the other cooing that they were their Aunty Marianne and Uncle Rolf.

Holding Gytha in his arms, Gilbert said, 'Can I have a proper welcome now?' He bent to kiss his wife.

'Would you like to meet Lady Camille?'

Gilbert did not let her finish. 'Not another one,' he said.

'I was about to say Lady Camille Hinds. Even I would have found it hard to produce three, Gilbert.'

'It's good to be back. If I ever have to leave again, you will have to travel with me.' Gytha smiled agreement. He was home, and she never wanted him to leave.

All was well. They were enemies united by love. Gytha and Enid attended to Marianne one month later as she married Rolf, a Norman maid and a Norman knight. But it was the marriages of Gytha and Gilbert and Enid and Gunter, both Saxon and Norman, and others like them throughout England that brought peace and harmony back, enemies united.

CPSIA information can be obtained
at www.ICGtesting.com
Printed in the USA
BVHW072223050421
604238BV00001B/43